PLAY AND LEARN

WITH

CEREAL O's

Language, Math, and Science

BOOKS BY TALITA PAOLINI

Read, Write, & Spell:
A Complete Guide for Home Education

Letter of the Day:
Fun Alphabet Activities for 3–5 year olds

PLAY AND LEARN

WITH

CEREAL O's

Language, Math, and Science

TALITA PAOLINI

Paolini International LLC
Livingston, Montana USA

Published by Paolini International LLC
P. O. Box 343
Livingston, MT 59047
U.S.A.

Visit us online: paolinimethod.com

Manufactured in the United States of America
Third Edition

**Publisher's Cataloging-In-Publication Data
(Prepared by The Donohue Group, Inc.)**

Names: Paolini, Talita.
Title: Play and learn with cereal O's : language, math, and science / Talita Paolini.
Other Titles: Play & learn with cereal O's
Description: Third edition. | Livingston, Montana : Paolini International LLC,
    [2019] | "Paolini Method, learning by doing"--Cover. | For parents and
    educators of 3-6 year old children.
Identifiers: ISBN 9780966621372
Subjects: LCSH: Education, Preschool--Activity programs. | Creative activities and
    seatwork. | English language--Study and teaching
    (Preschool) --Activity programs. | Mathematics--Study and teaching
    (Preschool) --Activity programs. | Science--Study and teaching
    (Preschool) --Activity programs.
Classification: LCC LB1140.35.C74 P36 2018 | DDC 372.21--dc23

Cover design by Tara Mayberry: TeaberryCreative.com
Author photo by Immanuela Meijer

In memory of my father,
Duane Neil Hodgkinson,
who once jumped over a house
to prove that (almost) nothing is impossible.

CONTENTS

❧ PREFACE ❧

The idea wouldn't go away. What if parents had a book that showed them exactly how to use a common, inexpensive item—such as breakfast cereal—to teach their children basic skills? What if the lessons gave parents a way to bond with their children while doing fun activities? Projects tumbled through my mind. When I had outlined twenty-five, I knew that I could no longer ignore the idea and this book was born.

My interest in education began in my early twenties when I trained as a Montessori preschool teacher. Following the birth of my first child, Christopher, I retired from teaching to concentrate on nurturing him. Watching him grow inspired me to develop simple projects to meet his needs. The expensive materials of the Montessori system were not practical for home use—and classroom techniques often didn't apply to a single student—so I was forced to develop lessons that fit our situation.

Two years later Angela was born. By the age of three, both children were doing first grade work. My husband, Kenneth, and I had to decide whether to put them in school with students their own age—where they would undoubtedly become bored—or keep teaching them at home. We decided to continue our adventure and homeschool through grade twelve.

Christopher and Angela finished high school early, at ages fifteen and fourteen respectively. Christopher went on to write the New York Times best-selling Inheritance Cycle and Angela has authored several screenplays. Thanks to an education that emphasized a love of learning, they still enjoy seeking out new knowledge.

Most of the lessons in this book are based on ones we did with our youngsters. Our family benefited so much from this method that we wanted to share these tools with other parents and caregivers.

If you are looking for a way to give your preschool or kindergarten child a great education but are unsure what to do or worry that the cost is prohibitive, this book can help! It shows you how to teach your child basic skills to prepare her for school and life.

Each activity has a specific educational goal. The projects progress through language and math in order. By working through these sections sequentially, you can easily teach the fundamentals of reading, writing, and math.

The lessons require only paper, colored markers, glue, scissors, cereal O's, and a few other common household items. Easy-to-understand directions and illustrations show you step-by-step how to make and use the materials so you'll know just what to do.

Whether you are a parent, caretaker of young children, grandparent, or a preschool teacher looking for new ideas, this book is for you!

Wishing you many happy hours of shared learning adventures with the little ones in your care,

Talita Paolini

✧ GETTING STARTED ✧

Welcome to an exciting program that shows you how to use cereal O's to teach your child the basics of math, reading, writing, and other essential skills. You can use the book in two ways: as a guide for teaching the fundamentals of language and math or as a resource for individual learning projects. Each lesson begins with a list of items required to complete it. If you need to prepare a material, instructions are provided. The heart of each project is called Activity, which tells you step-by-step how to present the lesson.

The book starts with language. The first three projects develop coordination, improve concentration, and help strengthen the fingers in preparation for holding a pencil. The letters and their sounds are introduced next with Letter Booklets. Your child is then shown how to string sounds together and begin writing. During this process, he will discover how to decode words and begin to read.

The math activities progress in similar fashion. Your child first works with Number Strips to see, compare, and count quantities of items 1–10. Next he makes Number Cards, which he uses to learn how to write numbers, associate them with objects, and then discover the fundamentals of addition, subtraction, multiplication, and division.

The final lessons focus on science, with an introduction to weight and balance, observing and charting data, weather, the solar system, and levers.

Helpful hints for using the *Play and Learn with Cereal O's* activities

- Your child's ability to learn new concepts expands as his brain matures, so observe his attention level as you present the lessons. If he has little interest in an activity, don't force him to do it but reintroduce it at a later time. If he shows high interest, allow him to repeat it as many times as he likes.

- Some projects, such as Lesson 4: Letter Booklets, are done over days or weeks. Others are completed in one session. Keep work periods short to keep enthusiasm high.

- With each project, first demonstrate the activity, then invite him to do it himself. Encourage his efforts with a cheerful attitude and be patient with his attempts. It is perfectly normal for youngsters to need a new concept presented several times before they learn it. Remember, information and ideas you take for granted are new to young children.

- Balance freedom of exploration and creativity with firm boundaries of behavior. Do this by demonstrating how to handle the materials carefully. Remove them if he is careless or destructive. Store project items away from toys to keep them safe.

A Few More Thoughts

- Books open a world of knowledge and adventure that is vital to your child's future education, work, and happiness. Read to him often to help him discover the pleasure of a good story and the joy of learning new things. Look at the pictures together and show him how to turn the pages gently. Give the books a home—in a box, bag, or on a shelf—so they are not scattered on the floor. Visit the library often to renew your supply.

- Help your child form booklets of his own art and writings. Staple pages of his work together under a colorful construction paper cover and have him "read" them to you.

- Engage him in conversation by asking questions about his feelings, likes and dislikes, and interests. Listen to what he tells you and share your thoughts in return.

A Note of Caution
Show young children exactly how cereal O's are used. Supervise closely so they don't put them into their nose or ears.

Downloadable Content: Visit my website to find illustrations and writing paper to accompany some of the lessons in this book:

paolinimethod.com/downloads

- Alphabet Pictures, large

- Alphabet Pictures, small

- Short Vowel Word Pictures, large

- Large writing paper: ⅞-inch-rule

Now turn to Lesson 1 and begin your adventure!

✌ LANGUAGE ✌

It's easy to teach your child how to read and write! Just follow these steps.

Step 1: Improve coordination and strengthen fingers

Lessons 1–3 introduce the three-finger grip, which strengthens the fingers in preparation for writing.

Step 2: Learn the letters' shapes and sounds

Lessons 4–5 help your child recognize and say the sounds of the letters. Tracing letter shapes with her fingers prepares her for writing.

Step 3: Begin writing and learn to blend letter sounds

Lessons 6–8 show your child how to write the letters and how to string two and three letter sounds together. During this phase, she may begin to read.

Step 4: Practice reading and writing

Lessons 9–11 provides beginning reading and writing practice. And she learns to write her name.

Once your child can read simple words, make her lots of one-word booklets. When she is comfortable with those, introduce ones with one sentence and later one paragraph per page. Begin with words she can easily sound out and then gradually add ones of increasing complexity. Encourage her to read the booklets to family and friends, and be sure to praise her efforts.

Next, teach her letter combinations that together make different sounds. Here are some examples: *thin, ship, rain, bean, ripe, boat, mule, light, wrap* and *knee*. Give her reasons to write every day, then gather her work into little books of her own.

Remember to visit your library often to provide a stream of fresh reading material. Develop a habit of reading with your child daily, and she will look forward to these times when you share adventures and learn fascinating new things together.

⁓ 1 ⁓

POSIE O'S

This activity helps your child improve hand-eye coordination and strengthen his fingers in preparation for writing, all while creating a pretty picture.

☞ What You Need:

Bowl of cereal O's, colored construction paper, colored markers, white glue, colored yarn (optional)

✄ To Prepare:

Use the colored markers to draw a large flower on the construction paper.

☆ Activity:

1. (Optional) Help your child glue colored yarn—green stem, yellow center, pink petals—over the flower outline. Let dry.

2. Demonstrate how to pick up and glue each cereal O carefully within the outlined petals. Invite your child to continue the activity. Encourage him to pinch each cereal O between the thumb and first two fingers. These are the fingers used to hold a pencil, so practicing this grip strengthens them in preparation for writing.

3. Let the picture dry and display it on a wall.

SPOON CHALLENGE

This fun game helps your child develop coordination and concentration by carrying increasing numbers of cereal O's on a spoon. It also satisfies her need to be active. To build finger strength for writing, encourage her to hold the spoon as she would a pencil.

☞ **What You Need:**

Cereal O's, two bowls, spoon (teaspoon or soup spoon)

✄ **To Prepare:**

1. Set a bowl of cereal O's on a table. Place a spoon next to the bowl.

2. Place an empty bowl on a table across the room or in a different room.

☆ **Activity:**

Demonstrate, then invite your child to follow the steps below. Encourage her to grip the spoon with her thumb and first two fingers:

1. Lift the spoon and hold it steady in front of you. Count one cereal O into the spoon.

2. Slowly and carefully walk to the second bowl and pour in the cereal O.

3. Return to the first bowl and repeat, this time counting out and carrying two pieces.

4. Continue adding the number of cereal O's to the spoon each trip. If a piece drops, either pick it up, place it in the spoon, and continue . . . or end the game.

Variation 1:

Carry cereal O's in larger or smaller spoons, or in other kitchen utensils.

Variation 2:

Place a sheet of paper and a crayon or marker by the far bowl. Each time cereal O's are successfully carried and dropped into the bowl, mark the number of O's on the paper. Young children make tally lines; older children write the numbers.

⚬ 3 ⚬

FRAME IT!

Making this project helps develop concentration and muscular control. Cereal O's give the frame a rustic, pebbly effect. Invite your child to build a set of three or make one as a gift for a friend.

☞ What You Need:

Bowl of cereal O's, eight craft or popsicle sticks, white glue, 4¼- by 4¼-inch picture, glitter and newspaper (optional)

☆ Activity:

Have your child follow these steps:

1. Glue double sets of craft sticks together at the ends. Let dry.

2. Glue cereal O's onto the craft stick frame. Be sure to hold the cereal between the first two fingers and thumb, as you would hold a pencil. Let dry.

3. Draw or choose a 4¼- by 4¼-inch picture of a person, thing, or animal. Glue the drawing or picture to the back of the frame and let it dry. For more stability, glue the picture on a piece of sturdy paper or cardboard before gluing it to the frame. Hang on a wall to display.

Variation:

Place the frame (with glued-on cereal O's) on a tray or newspaper. Demonstrate, then have your child drizzle white glue over the O's and sprinkle them with glitter. Let dry. Shake off excess glitter and display. Be sure to supervise this activity closely so he doesn't eat any glitter.

❧ 4 ❧

LETTER BOOKLETS

This important activity is your child's first step toward reading and writing. As she builds Letter Booklets, she will learn to identify the letters, trace them, and say their sounds. Collect finished booklets in a basket for use in the following lessons: Trace and Write: Letters, Five Special Friends, and Build-a-Word.

☞ What You Need:

Bowl of cereal O's, three sheets blue construction paper, eleven sheets red construction paper, thick black marker, white glue, tape, scissors, Alphabet Pictures–large (page 12) or other pictures of your choice

✄ To Prepare:

1. Cut the blue and red construction paper in half. Fold the pieces in half and crease firmly to form 5 blue and 21 red Letter Booklets.

2. Write a large letter a on the cover and right interior page of one blue Letter Booklet. Repeat with the letters *e, i, o, u* on the remaining blue booklets. These letters are vowels. When you write, try to make the letters' lines straight and the curves consistently round.

3. Write the letters *b, c, d, f, g, h, j, k, l, m, n, p, q, r, s, t, v, w, x, y,* and *z* on the covers and insides of twenty-one red Letter Booklets. These are consonants.

☆ Activity 1:

1. Begin with the letter *a.* Trace the letter on the cover with your finger and say its sound, *a*—as in <u>a</u>pple (A Word About Letter Sounds, page 24).

Make sure to trace the letter as you would write it (Verbal Cues, page 28). For example, the letter *t* is traced with a down line, then crossed from left to right. Invite your child to trace the letter and say its sound.

2. Open the Letter Booklet, apply a thick line of glue over the letter, then have her press cereal O's into the glue.

3. Set the Letter Booklet aside to dry.

Note: Build one or more Letter Booklets each day. Keep them in a basket for Activities 2–3 and other projects. Encourage your child to look at the Letter Booklets and say their sounds often.

☆ **Activity 2:**

1. Choose a Letter Booklet and open it to show the cereal O's letter.

2. Trace the shape of the cereal O's letter and say its sound. Again, make sure to trace the letter as you would write it. Do this two times. Invite your child to repeat your actions.

3. Choose another letter and repeat. Do this activity with one or more letters each day until she can trace the letters and say their sounds by herself.

☆ **Activity 3:**

Invite your child to choose a Letter Booklet. Have her trace it and say its sound. Together, name things that begin with that letter's sound. Cut and paste an Alphabet Picture or draw an illustration of your own on the left inside page of the booklet. Here are some picture ideas:

a—apple, ant, accordion, alligator, ax, anchor, antler, animals, ankle
b—butterfly, basket, banana, bear, bed, bat, bunny, barn, boot, box, bell
c—cow, car, corn, cat, camera, crayon, candle, cactus, cup, candy, camel
d—dime, deer, duck, dog, dragon, door, doll, dad, dolphin, dollar, desk
e—egg, elephant, engine, elk, elbow, elf, emerald, elevator, energy
f—flag, flower, fish, fern, fork, fire, fairy, fender, father, fur, finger, four
g—goat, glass, golf ball, grapes, grasshopper, guitar, goose, globe, glove
h—horse, hoe, helicopter, hand, hammer, hat, hen, harp, honey, hose, hut
i—insect, ink, iguana, Indian, igloo, impala, inch, infant, Italy, India
j—jet, jacket, jam, jellybeans, jade, Jupiter, jeep, jump rope, jeans, juice

k—key, kangaroo, ketchup, kite, kitten, kimono, kettle, kitchen, kelp
l—lettuce, lizard, lion, lemon, leaf, ladybug, lamp, ladder, lamb, lips
m—money, map, monkey, mushroom, mustard, mirror, marble, mouth
n—nut, newspaper, needle, nickel, nest, necklace, napkin, noodle, nose
o—octopus, octagon, olive, otter, ostrich, ox, ocelot
p—popcorn, plate, pillow, plane, pepper, pig, peach, penguin, puppy, pizza
q—quilt, queen, quartz, quail, question mark, quarter, quiver, quart
r—rock, rug, river, red, ring, rabbit, radish, ribbon, rooster, rose, rat, rice
s—snake, snow, sunflower, sun, skirt, snowman, sand, soap, star, swan
t—table, tub, tiger, teaspoon, telephone, toast, tree, toad, tent, train, tape
u—umbrella, underwear, up, under, uncle, undershirt
v—velvet, Venus, volcano, violin, vanilla, vacuum, violet, vest, vase, vine
w—wood, walrus, watermelon, wing, worm, window, water, wire, walnut
x—ax, wax, ox, box, fox
y—yarn, yellow, yam, yeast, yawn, year, yak, yard, yogurt, yolk, yes, yo-yo
z—zebra, zero, zoo, zipper, zinnia, zigzag, zither, zucchini

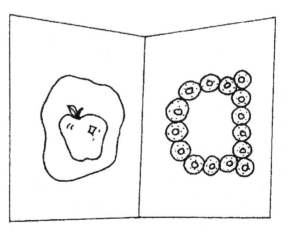

A Word About Letter Sounds

Each letter has a name *and* one or more sounds. The letter *b*, for example, has the *name bee*, but its *sound* is short and explosive without any following vowel tone. (You can hear the letter sounds on my website: www.paolinimethod.com/downloads) Teach your child the names of the letters, *Aee, Bee, Cee*, etc., but emphasize the phonetic *sounds* of the letters and she will soon be able to decipher words.

Each vowel *(a, e, i, o, u)* represents two or more sounds. Notice the *a* in *cat, cake,* and *father.* To simplify, teach your child the *short* sound of each vowel, as demonstrated by these words: *cat, hen, sit, hop, hut.* This will give her the tools to begin reading simple words and sentences.

When you say the consonants (all the letters that are not the vowels—*a, e, i, o, u*), try to say just the *sound* of the letter. In our *b* example, say the word *bat.* Now say the *b* sound without the *at* that follows. The letters *b, c, d, g, j, k, p,* and *t* have short, explosive sounds. Try isolating their sounds in these words: *bat, cat, dig, gun, jam, kitten, pin,* and *top.* The sound for letter *h* is also short, but it is quietly exhaled as in *hat.* Another short sound is *y.* Say it as in *yarn.*

The sounds for *f, l, m, n, r, s, v, w,* and *z* are held longer. Say them as the first sound in the words *fox, lamp, mop, nut, run, sit, vase, window,* and *zebra.* The letter *q* is always followed by *u* and is said *kw,* as in *quiet.* The letter *x* combines two sounds and is said *ks* as in *fox.*

Note: Once your child is comfortable and confident with short vowel words, introduce other vowel sounds formed by two or more letters, such as *cake, rain, hay, feed, seal, key, time, high, fly, home, boat, snow, mule, fuel,* and *new.* Beginning readers can also learn that letters such as *c* and *g* have more than one sound—as in *cap* and *cent* and in *get* and *gem*—and that consonant pairs make different sounds, as in *ship, chess, think, when, knife,* and *phone.*

HELLO *a!*

This wonderful collection of pre-reading games reinforces the letters' sounds (A Word About Letter Sounds, page 24). Spend a few minutes playing them daily and soon the letters will be friends that your child recognizes instantly.

☞ What You Need:
Letter Booklets (page 20)

☆ Activity 1:

1. Set out the *a* Letter Booklet. Say, "Hello *a!*" Set out the *b, c, d,* and *e* Letter Booklets in a row. Greet each one: "Hello *b,* Hello *c,*" etc.

2. Once five Letter Booklets are presented, dramatically "open the door" of the *a* booklet and say, *"a* is for . . . *apple!*" Repeat with each of the other letters, pretending that each one holds a mystery that you rediscover every time you "open the door."

3. Once all five booklets are open, point to one and say, for example, "Can you trace the *d* and say its sound, *d?*" Make sure he traces the letter as if he were writing it (Verbal Cues, page 28). Repeat with the other four letters.

4. Now ask him to close each booklet. Say, "It's time to close the doors now. Can you please close the *c* door?" Repeat until all are closed.

5. Finally say, "It's time for our letter friends to go home. Goodbye *a!*" Pick up the a Letter Booklet. Wave goodbye to it together as you put it in its "home"—a basket or box. Repeat with each of the remaining letters.

6. If his interest level is still high, set out a new set of Letter Booklets and follow step 1–5. Repeat Activity 1 as a game over many days, weeks, or months until he knows each letter's sound.

☆ Activity 2:

1. Do this activity once your child is proficient with Activity 1. Set out part, half, or all of the Letter Booklets in rows on the floor. Sit across the room with the Letter Booklet basket.

2. Say, "Mark, can you bring me *f*?" When he brings the *f* Letter Booklet, thank him and place it in the basket.

3. Continue asking for letters until all the Letter Booklets have been brought. Keep the activity fun. If he makes a mistake, note that he needs more practice and review the letter another time.

☆ Activity 3:

1. Place the letters into a bag or upside down in a container different from their "home." Place the empty Letter Booklet basket across the room or in a different part of the house.

2. Explain that the Letter Booklets have been taking a vacation, but now they are coming home. Take them out one at a time and say, "What is this?" Your child answers, "This is *r.*" You say, "Can you please take *r* home?" He then carries the booklet to its home basket. Repeat with the other letters.

ᐩ 6 ᐩ

TRACE AND WRITE: LETTERS

In this lesson, your child learns how to write the letters. Keep the activity fun by doing one to three letters per day in short sessions. Praise her efforts and watch her writing skills improve.

☞ **What You Need:**

Letter Booklets (page 20), lined writing paper (page 12), pencil

Note: If you don't have Letter Booklets, draw large letters on slips of paper and substitute.

☆ **Activity:**

1. Choose one Letter Booklet. Open it to show the cereal O's letter.

2. With your child observing, trace over the cereal O's letter with your fingers in the same pattern you would write it, while saying its verbal cue (see next page). Then say the letter's sound (A Word About Letter Sounds, page 24). With the letter *b,* for example, say, "down, up and around" as you write it. Then say its sound, *b.* Invite her to trace the letter and say its sound two times herself.

3. Demonstrate how to write the letter on lined paper. Do this slowly, so she can see how it is formed. Point out that it sits on the line. Ask her to write the letter several times herself.

Note: Help your beginning writer by making dashed-line letters for her to trace with a pencil.

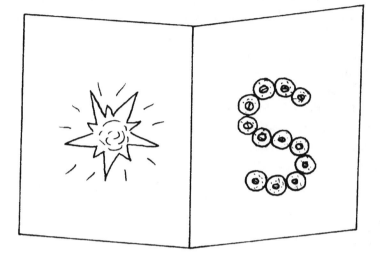

Verbal Cues:

Once your child associates these directional cues with the letters, she will always remember how to form them. Note that the hand written shapes of *a* and *g* differ noticeably from the printed font shown below:

a—up and around, up, down
b—down, up and around
c—up and around
d—up and around, up, down
e—across, up and around
f—curve, straight down, across
g—up and around, up, down and curve
h—down, up, over and down
i—down, dot
j—down, curve, dot
k—down, slant, slant
l—down
m—down, up and over, down, up and over, down
n—down, up and over, down
o—up and around
p—down, up and around
q—up and around, up, down
r—down, up and over
s—up and curve and curve again
t—down and across
u—down, curve, up, down
v—slant down, slant up
w—slant down, slant up, slant down, slant up
x—slant, slant
y—slant, big slant
z—across, slant, across

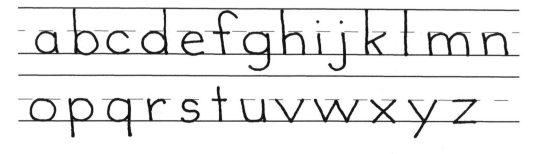

How to Hold a Pencil:

Pinch the pencil with the thumb and first finger just above the line where the paint meets the sharpened wood tip. Let the pencil rest on the first joint of the middle finger, as shown below. This is called the three-fingered grip. Left-handers use a similar position but should grip the pencil a bit higher so they can see over and around their hand.

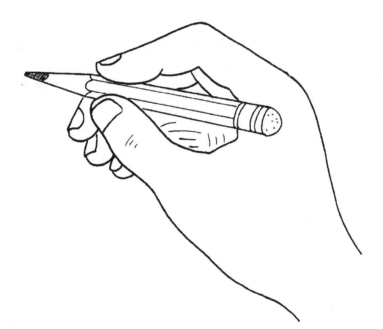

ॐ 7 ॐ

FIVE SPECIAL FRIENDS

Do this lesson as soon as your child knows the sounds of the letters. Repeat Activity 1 often—over days or weeks—until he is comfortable saying the vowel sounds. When he is ready, introduce Activity 2 and repeat it over many days until he can blend two letters easily. Activity 3 blends three letters. At this point many children suddenly understand that the blended sounds represent real things. For example, the letters c-a-t mean cat!

☞ **What You Need:**

Letter Booklets (page 20) or separate slips of paper with letters written on them

☆ **Activity 1:**

Demonstrate, then invite your child to follow these steps:

1. Set the five blue Letter Booklets *(a, e, i, o, u)* in a vertical line, as shown on the next page. These are the Five Special Friends.

2. Point to the letters and say their sounds, one-by-one, starting with a. (A Word About Letter Sounds, page 24). Repeat this several times.

Another day, challenge your child to say the vowel sounds in order with his eyes closed.

☆ **Activity 2:**

1. Ask your child to set out the vowels in a vertical line.

2. Invite him to get a consonant and place it in front of the *a*. Let's say he chooses the letter *b*. Blend the *b* and the *a* sounds and say *ba (baaa)*. Now move the *b* booklet down to rest in front of the *e*. Say *be* (as in the word *bed)*. Continue moving the *b* down until you reach *u*. You will have said *ba, be, bi, bo, bu*. Have him try the exercise himself.

3. Tell him put the *b* away, then have him choose a new consonant and repeat action 2.

☆ **Activity 3:**

1. Ask your child to set out the vowels in a vertical line, as before.

2. Have him choose one consonant, for example *b,* and place it to the left of the vowel, as he did in Activity 2.

3. Introduce a third letter, such as *t*. Place it to the right of the vowel. With your child, move both consonants down the vowels and say the blended sounds: *bat, bet, bit, bot, but*. Blend the sounds as if you were reading the words. Choose other consonants and repeat.

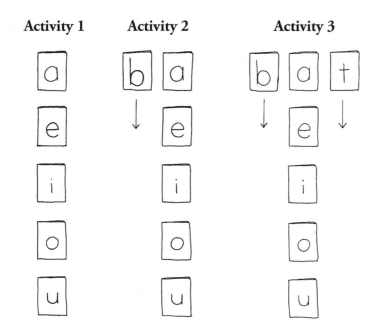

౽ 8 ౽

BUILD ≉ A ≉ WORD

Like Five Special Friends, this activity is a precursor to reading. Children will usually begin to decipher words as they work with the lesson.

☞ What You Need:

Letter Booklets (page 20) or separate slips of paper with letters written on them, items or pictures that represent simple words (short vowel word pictures, page 12), lined writing paper (page 12), construction paper, stapler, pencil

☆ Activity 1:

1. Invite your child to place the Letter Booklets on the floor or on a table.

2. Set out an item or picture of a simple word. Say the individual sounds of the word, such as, "This is *c-a-t*." Ask her to find the three Letter Booklets *c, a,* and *t* and place them next to the picture.

3. Together, say each letter's sound and the word. "This is *c-a-t, cat.*"

4. Choose a new picture or item and repeat steps 2 and 3. Build *a* words one day, *e* words another, and so forth. If a word requires a double letter, simply write the additional one on a slip of paper.

☆ Activity 2:

Cut lined writing paper in half to create small pages. Invite your child to repeat Activity 1, but this time have her print the words on the prepared paper. Gather the pages into little books (one for each vowel), cut construction paper covers, and staple down the sides. Title them in this fashion:

Angela's *a* words, Jason's *e* words, Marvin's *i* words, Abbie's *o* words, Irene's *u* words, etc. Encourage her to read the booklets to family and friends.

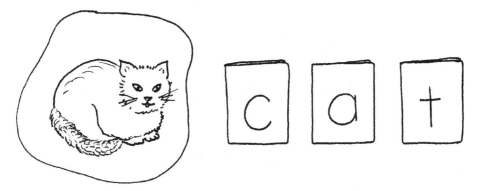

Here is a list of simple words for each vowel:

a **words:** and, ant, ask, bag, bat, can, cap, cat, dad, fan, fat, gas, ham, hat, jam, lad, lap, man, map, nap, pan, rag, ran, rat, sad, sat, van, wag, wax, yam, zap, back, camp, crab, flag, hand, lamp, last, pant, plan, rack, raft, sand, sack, snap, black, class, drank, grass, plant, quack, snack, stamp, track

e **words:** bed, beg, den, fed, get, hen, jet, led, leg, men, met, net, peg, pen, pet, ten, vet, wet, yes, bell, belt, best, deck, dent, desk, fell, fled, left, melt, mess, neck, nest, peck, pest, rest, send, sled, stem, step, tell, tent, test, vest, well, went, west, yell, blend, dress, glass, grass, press, seven, smell, spend

i **words:** it, bib, dig, fig, fin, ink, kid, lid, pig, pin, pit, rib, rim, rip, tin, wig, yip, zip, crib, dill, fill, fist, gift, gill, grin, hill, hilt, kiss, lint, list, milk, mill, mint, mist, mitt, pill, pink, silk, spin, tick, twig, twin, wick, wink, blimp, blink, brick, drill, drink, grill, prick, quill, quilt, stick, trick, kitten, mitten

o **words:** on, box, cob, cop, cot, dog, dot, fog, fox, hog, hop, hot, job, log, lot, mom, mop, pop, pot, sob, top, blob, cost, doll, drop, frog, honk, lock, lost, moss, plot, pond, rock, sock, stop, toss, block, clock, cross, flock, floss, frond, smock, stomp, locket, pocket, rocket, pompom

u **words:** up, bud, bug, bun, bus, cub, cup, dug, gum, gun, hum, hut, mud, nun, nut, pup, rub, rug, rum, run, sun, tub, tug, buck, bunk, club, drug, drum, duck, dump, dust, grub, gull, hump, jump, lump, muff, plug, plus, pump, rust, slug, crust, truck, skunk, stump, muffin, pumpkin, trumpet

❧ 9 ❧

FRIENDS OF *a* BOOKLET

This project provides great practice for a beginning reader. Words that have the same vowels are grouped together as "friends" into little books. Your child may enjoy helping make the booklets in the optional writing activity.

☞ **What You Need:**

Cereal O's, fourteen sheets white 8½- by 11-inch paper, three pieces 8½- by 11-inch construction paper, colored markers, scissors, stapler, glue, red and blue pencils (optional)

✂ **To Prepare: Booklets**

1. Cut two pieces of construction paper into quarters to make eight smaller pieces. You will use five of these to make covers for the Friends of *a, e, i, o,* and *u* Booklets. Keep one sheet whole.

2. Cut thirteen sheets of plain white paper into quarters. These will form the pages of the booklets. You will have one piece of paper remaining uncut.

3. Gather five sets of ten white paper pages. Put a colored construction paper cover on each set and staple along the short side to form five booklets.

4. With blue marker, write one vowel *(a, e, i, o, u)* on the cover of each booklet.

5. Use colored markers to write one simple word on each page of the booklets (sample words on page 33). Write the letters large, making the consonants red and the vowels blue.

✂ To Prepare: Reading Chart

To make the Cereal O's Reading Chart, take the remaining piece of uncut white paper and cut it into a 5- by 10-inch rectangle. Draw four vertical and nine horizontal lines to form 1-inch squares. Decorate the bottom square of each column with a starburst of colored-marker lines, making each one a different color. Glue the chart onto the third sheet of construction paper, aligning the bottom edges as shown below. Write *a, e, i, o, u* above the sets of squares. Attach the Cereal O's Reading Chart to a wall or refrigerator.

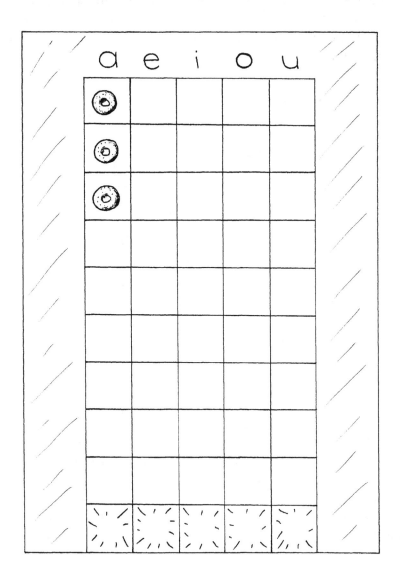

☆ **Activity 1:**

1. Ask your child to choose a booklet, trace the letter on the cover with his fingers, and say the sound of the vowel. Open the booklet. Coach him to say the sounds, then say the full word: *h-e-n, hen.* If he can read the words easily, eliminate the sounding-out part.

2. Invite him to read you a booklet each day, beginning with the Friends of *a.* Each time he reads all ten pages, he glues a cereal O onto his Cereal O's Reading Chart. When he has read the booklet ten times, he glues a cereal O onto the starburst square and begins a new booklet. You may wish to add an additional incentive or treat for the completion of each column or the entire chart.

☆ **Activity 2:**

Prepare another set of five booklets (using new words), as instructed on page 34, except this time write one word on each page with lead pencil. Have your child trace over your letters with colored pencils, using blue for vowels and red for consonants. Do all or part of a booklet daily, working in short sessions to keep the project fun. Invite him to read you his finished work, and congratulate him on his efforts.

❧ 10 ❧

WRITING MY NAME

Your child's name is very special to her. Learning to form and write it gives her a sense of accomplishment and pride. Encourage her to write her name often on artwork, with a stick in sand, at the bottom of letters to relatives, with finger paint, in mud, in cake frosting . . . everywhere!

☞ **What You Need:**

Letter Booklets (page 20) or separate slips of paper with letters written on them, lined writing paper (page 12), lead pencil

For the Variation on the next page, you'll also need construction paper, colored pencils, and scissors

☆ **Activity 1: Building My Name**

1. Show your child how to assemble the Letter Booklets to form her name. If it requires extra letters, simply write them on slips of paper.

2. Mix up the letters and have her try to reform her name.

☆ **Activity 2: Writing My Name**

1. Have your child build her name with the Letter Booklets.

2. Demonstrate how to write her name on the lined paper. Write slowly so she can see how the letters are formed and say the sound of each letter as you print it. Ask her to copy her name several times.

Variation:

Invite your child to make a rainbow name book. Cut writing paper in half to create seven small pages and provide seven colored pencils (to match the rainbow colors). Have her print her name several times on each sheet using a different colored pencil for each page. When all the pages are done, cut a construction paper cover and staple the stack together at the side. Title it *"My Name Book."*

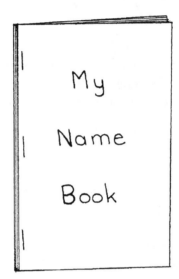

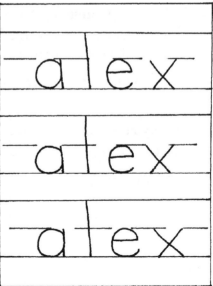

✌ 11 ✌

STORY O'S

This engaging project is fun for children who can write and also for prewriters. For nonwriters, the activity improves visual discrimination, improves coordination, and strengthens the three-finger grip used to hold a pencil. For students who can write, the lesson invites them to invent a whimsical story and decorate it creatively.

☞ What You Need:

Bowl of cereal O's, lined writing paper (page 12), pencil, glue

Note: This activity is presented in two ways: to nonwriters and to writers.

✂ To Prepare: Nonwriter

Invent a short story or poem—or choose a few lines from a book—and write it on lined paper. Print the letters so the *o*'s are the same size as cereal O's.

☆ Activity: Nonwriter

1. Read the story to your child.

2. Have him glue the cereal O's over the *o*'s in the story. Encourage him to hold the cereal with his first two fingers and thumb while he does this, in preparation for holding a pencil.

Variation:

Have your child trace each *o* with a pencil before gluing on the cereal O.

✄ To Prepare: Writer

Same as above, except your child writes the story himself.

☆ Activity: Writer

1. Invite your child to make up a story or offer him a sentence or paragraph to copy. Have him write it and then read it to you. Encourage him to read it to his friends and family members.

2. Have him glue cereal O's over the *o*'s he has written and decorate it.

Here are some story ideas:

1. Write about things that are round: tires, balls, balloons, frisbees, turtles, doughnuts, cookies, eyeglasses, bowls, etc.

2. Write about a subject that has an *o* in it: *frog, octopus, olive, doll, rock, mom, dog, hog, locket, Tom, clock, pond, fox, sock, pompom, blocks, mop.*

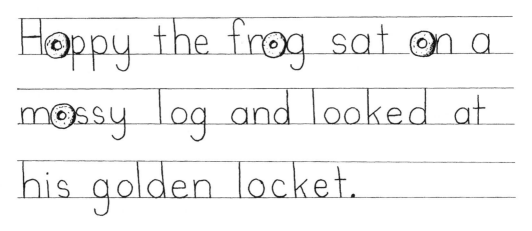

✣ MATH ✣

Counting and grouping movable objects is the best way to introduce the basics of math. Cereal O's are perfect for this purpose!

Step 1: Introduce the concept of quantity
>   Lesson 12 demonstrates the amounts that the numbers 1–10 represent and helps your child understand the relationship between those numbers.

Step 2: Learn to write the numbers and associate them with things
>   Lessons 13–14 show how to identify and write number symbols and associate them with a quantity of cereal O's.

Step 3: Practice counting
>   Lessons 15–20 offer lots of fun counting practice.

Step 4: Discover addition, subtraction, multiplication, and division
>   Lessons 21–24 give hands-on experience with the four basic mathematical operations.

Use daily life situations to introduce your child to numbers. Count apples in a fruit bowl, flowers on a plant, cars on the street, pencils and pens, napkins (as you put them on the table), along with windows, doors, and stairs in your home. Count fingers and toes and buttons on clothes. Once he learns to write numbers, he can jot down the quantities of things he counts, measure length, weigh items, chart daily temperature, etc.

Encourage play with measuring spoons and cups, pint and quart jars, and gallon containers. Ask questions about how many of one it takes to fill another and then let your child experiment to find the answers. Invite him to join you when measuring ingredients and show him how to double or halve a recipe.

Look for ways to make math interesting and enjoyable by pointing out how useful numbers are in daily life and how they help us understand the world.

ঞ 12 ঞ

INTRODUCING NUMBERS

This lesson helps your child learn the names of the numbers and understand their relationship to each other.

☞ What You Need:

Bowl of cereal O's, cardstock or cardboard, colored marker, scissors, white glue, basket or box

✂ To Prepare:

1. Cut the cardstock to make five Number Strips that are 1-inch wide and 10-inches long.

2. With colored marker, draw vertical lines at 1-inch intervals along the strips.

3. Set aside one Number Strip. This will be number 10. Cut the remaining strips to make numbers 1–9 (see illustrations).

4. To complete the material, glue one cereal O in each space and set aside to dry. Place in a basket or box for storage.

☆ Activity 1: Three-Part Naming Game

Present this three-step activity all at once or over days, according to your child's readiness.

Step 1: This Is . . .

Set out the Number Strips 1, 2, and 3. Say the name and count the cereal O's on each one as you set it down. "This is one. One. This is two. One, two. This is three. One, two, three." Next, mix up the strips and invite your child to repeat your actions. Follow this pattern with 4–10 now or at a later time.

This is two.

Step 2: Point to the . . .

Set out several Number Strips. Say one of the numbers and ask her to point to it. Mix the strips. Name a different one and ask her to point to it or hand it to you.

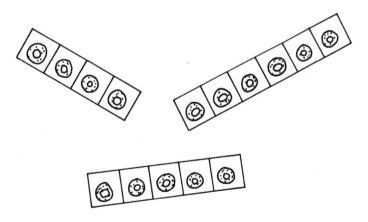

Point to six.

Step 3: What Is This?

Once your child is confident with Steps 1 and 2, set out the strips as before. This time, point to one and ask her to tell you its name. Say, "Katie, what is this?" When she can answer easily, she has mastered this activity.

When you are done with the material for the day, hand her each item while saying its name, and ask her to put it away in its box or basket. Encourage her to repeat the strip's name one final time as she puts it away.

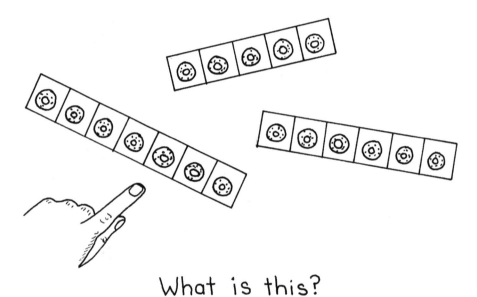

What is this?

Note:

If your child says an incorrect name in Step 3, observe where she needs more work, smile, and then put the project away. Another day, return to Steps 1 and 2 and present the lesson again. Be patient; repetition is an important part of learning.

Your role is not to criticize or correct but to help her learn for herself, to facilitate mastery through practice. (Adults often want to rush to the final step—to push the child to give the right answers when time would be better spent reinforcing the names in Step 2.) Only when you are sure she can correctly identify the items should you proceed to Step 3. Remember that every time she is successful, she builds confidence, which feeds her enthusiasm to learn more.

☆ **Activity 2:**

1. Set out the Number Strips at random.

2. Demonstrate how to find 1, count it, and then place before you. Next invite your child to find 2, count it, and set it directly above 1. Repeat with 3–10, counting and building upward as shown.

3. When all the Number Strips have been placed, ask her to count upward from 1–10, pointing at each strip in turn.

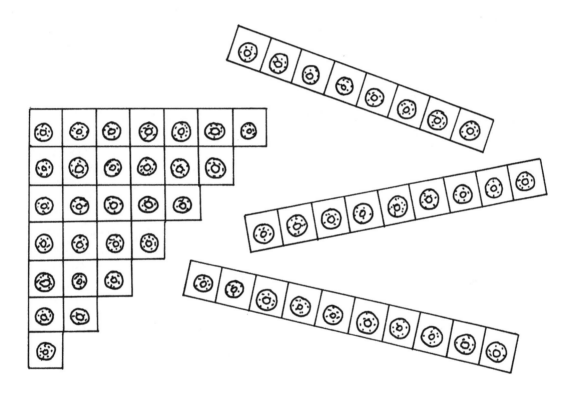

❧ 13 ❧

NUMBER CARDS

This project helps your child associate the names of the numbers with their symbols. Tracing the numerals with his fingers prepares him to write them, which he will do in the next lesson.

☞ **What You Need:**

Bowl of cereal O's, five sheets colored construction paper, thick black marker, white glue, tape, scissors, Number Strips (page 42)

✄ **To Prepare:**

1. Cut the construction paper in half to make ten pages.

2. On one page, use the marker to draw a large number 1 and write the word one beneath the number.

3. Repeat step 2 to make Number Cards 2–10.

Note: For an older child, make the numbers on quarter sheets of construction paper.

☆ **Activity 1: Building Number Cards**

1. Apply a thick line of glue over the number.

2. Invite your child to press cereal O's into the glue.

3. Set the Number Card aside to dry.

Note: Build one or more numbers each day and keep them in a basket for Activities 2–5. Review them often with your child.

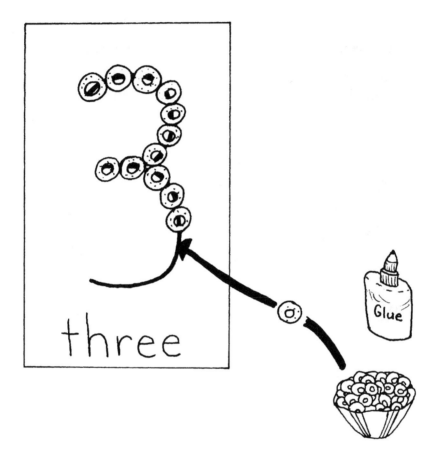

☆ **Activity 2: This Is . . .**

1. Choose a Number Card.

2. Trace the number with your fingers and say its name. Make sure to trace the number as you would write it. Do this two times. Invite your child to follow your example.

3. Choose another Number Card and repeat. Do this activity with a few Number Cards daily until he can trace them and say their names by himself.

☆ **Activity 3: Point to the . . .**

1. Lay three or more Number Cards on a table or carpet. Mix them up so they are not in numerical order.

2. Say the name of a number and ask your child to point to it.

3. Mix the Number Cards again and ask for a different number.

4. Repeat the activity using another set of Number Cards. Do this over days or weeks until he can easily identify the correct numbers.

Can you find six?

☆ **Activity 4: What Is This?**

1. Lay three or more Number Cards on a table or carpet. Mix them up so they are not in numerical order.

2. This time (instead of saying the name of the number) point to a Number Card and ask him to tell you its name.

3. Repeat the activity using a different set of Number Cards. If he has trouble with any of the names, put the lesson away and review Activities 2 and 3 at another time.

☆ Activity 5: Place in Order

1. 1. Put all the Number Cards at random on the floor.

2. Show your child how to find 1 and place it to the left, then set out 2, 3, 4, . . . 10, building to the right in sequential order.

3. Invite him to repeat the activity without your help.

☆ Activity 6: Match Quantity to Name

1. Set out the Number Cards in order from 1–10, as in Activity 5.

2. Below them, set out at random the Number Strips from Lesson 12. Ask him to choose a Number Strip, count the cereal O's, and then place it below the correct Number Card. Continue in like fashion until all the strips are matched with their associated numbers.

❧ 14 ❧

TRACE AND WRITE: NUMBERS

This simple activity gives your child practice writing the numbers 1–10. Point out that numbers sit on the line with their tops slightly below the line above them. Use the verbal cues on page 51. Write slowly when you demonstrate so she can see exactly how they are formed.

☞ **What You Need:**

Number Cards (page 46), lined writing paper, pencil

Note: If you don't have Number Cards, print the numerals 1–10 on slips of paper and substitute in the lesson.

☆ **Activity:**

1. Choose one Number Card.

2. Trace over the cereal O's number with your fingers in the same fashion you would write it. Say its name. Invite your child to do the same two times herself.

3. Write the number on lined paper, saying its verbal cue as you form it. Encourage her to practice writing it, along with its verbal cue, many times.

Note: Help your beginning writer by making dashed-line numbers for her to trace with her pencil.

Verbal Cues:

Use these directions to help your child remember how to form the numbers:

1—Make a line that goes straight down.
2—Curve and slant and then across.
3—Make a curve, then make another.
4—Down across and down again.
5—Down and curve, then across the top.
6—Make a curve, then circle the bottom.
7—Go across and then slant down.
8—Curve and curve and curve and curve.
9—Make a circle, then go straight down.
10—Go straight down, then make a circle.

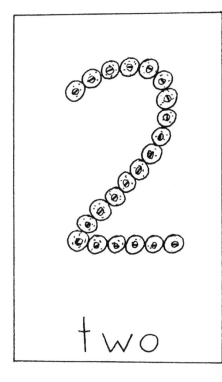

ꙮ 15 ꙮ

COUNT AND GLUE

Help your child associate the written numbers with separate items—cereal O's—with this fun project!

☞ **What You Need:**

Bowl of cereal O's, three sheets colored construction paper or card stock, colored markers, white glue, scissors, box or basket

✂ **To Prepare:**

1. Cut the three sheets of colored paper into quarters to make twelve pages.

2. Write the numbers 1–12 on the bottom of the pages, as shown in the illustration. Leave the upper part of the pages blank. (For a very young child, draw dots to indicate where he will glue on corresponding numbers of cereal O's.)

3. Set the Count and Glue pages upside down in a box or basket. Make sure they are in random order.

☆ **Activity 1:**

Demonstrate, then have your child follow these steps:

1. Choose a Count and Glue page.

2. Say the name of the number.

3. Count out the correct number of cereal O's and glue them on the sheet. A very young child will glue them on the prepared dots.

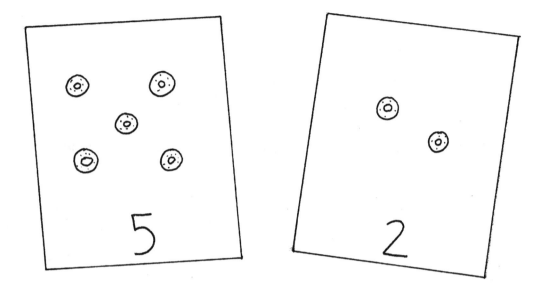

☆ **Activity 2:**

1. Ask your child to arrange the Count and Glue number pages from 1–12 on a table or carpet, and then say their names in order.

2. Invite him to trace the numbers with his fingers or with a pencil.

❧ 16 ❧

COUNTING GAME

Your child associates things with their corresponding numbers with this fun activity.

☞ **What You Need:**

Fifty-five cereal O's in a bowl, string or yarn, paper, colored marker, scissors, ruler

✂ **To Prepare:**

1. Cut ten 1½- by 1½-inch squares of paper.

2. Write the numbers 1–10 (one number on each paper square) to make Number Slips.

3. Cut a three-foot length of string or yarn.

☆ **Activity:**

Demonstrate, then have your child follow these steps:

1. Set the string horizontally on a table or carpet.

2. Place the Number Slips consecutively above the string, leaving spaces between them.

3. Set one cereal O under the number 1. Say, "One." Set two cereal O's under the number 2. As you set them out, say, "One, two. Two." Set three cereal O's under the number 3. As you set them out, say, "One, two, three. Three." Continue in like manner until all the cereal O's are placed.

4. Count across, pointing to each set.

Variation:
Substitute other small items for the cereal O's: buttons, pasta bows or shells, little toy figures, colored pom-pom balls, stickers on small squares of paper, pebbles, sea shells, small pine or fir cones. Supervise so your child doesn't place items in his mouth, nose, or ears.

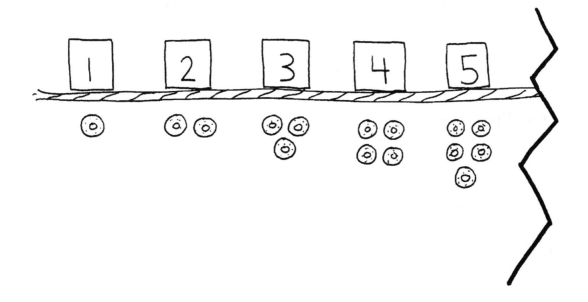

৵ 17 ৵

KERPLUNK:

READ, COUNT, AND DROP

Reinforce counting skills with this do-it-yourself game.

☞ What You Need:
Fifty-five cereal O's in a bowl, two additional bowls, paper, colored marker, scissors, ruler, chair

✂ To Prepare:
1. Cut eleven 2- by 3-inch pieces of paper. Fold them in half, short end to short end, to make Number Fold-Ups.

2. Write the numbers 0–10 (one number inside each Number Fold-Up) and put the papers in a bowl.

☆ Activity:
Demonstrate, then have your child follow these steps:

1. Place an empty bowl on the floor behind a straight-backed chair.

2. Choose a Number Fold-Up. Read it and set the paper aside.

3. Kneel on the chair facing backward. While holding the bowl of fifty-five cereal O's, count and drop the number of O's indicated by the Number Fold-Up into the bowl on the floor.

4. Take another Number Fold-Up and repeat. Tell your child that 0 means nothing and indicates that no cereal O's are dropped. When all the Number Fold-Ups are gone, all the cereal O's should be in the bowl on the floor.

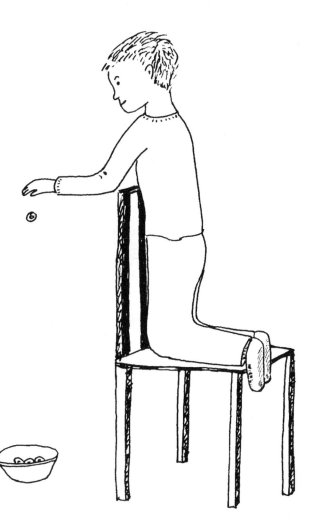

✂ 18 ✂

TOWER POWER

This exciting project combines counting practice with a hands-on building activity!

☞ **What You Need:**

Fifty-five cereal O's in a bowl, large marshmallows, toothpicks, plain paper or construction paper, colored markers, scissors, ruler

✂ **To Prepare:**

1. Cut ten 2- by 3-inch pieces of paper to make Number Slips.

2. Write the numbers 1–10 at the bottoms of the slips.

☆ **Activity:**

Demonstrate, then have your child follow these steps:

1. Place the ten Number Slips consecutively on a table, leaving spaces between them.

2. Set one marshmallow on each Number Slip. Stick a toothpick in the top of each marshmallow. (Be sure to supervise her with the toothpicks.)

3. Drop one cereal O onto the toothpick on Number Slip 1. Say, "One." Stack two cereal O's on the toothpick on Number Slip 2. As you drop them say, "One, two. Two." Put three cereal O's on the toothpick on Number Slip 3. As you drop them say, "One, two, three. Three." Continue stacking in like manner until all the cereal O's have been placed.

4. Count across 1–10, pointing to each set.

Variation 1:
Place the cereal O's next to each other on the Number Slips without using marshmallows and toothpicks.

Variation 2:
Stack the cereal O's on the Number Slips without using marshmallows and toothpicks. Building cereal O's ten high is very difficult, so once you stack five, begin a second pile of five.

༈ 19 ༈

EGG CARTON COUNTING GAME

This delightful project teaches the concept that numbers correspond to a specific quantity of items. Your child can play this self-correcting game all by himself. If he runs out of cereal O's or has some left at the end, he'll know that he didn't count correctly.

☞ What You Need:

Seventy-three cereal O's in a bowl, construction paper, empty egg carton, colored markers, scissors

✂ To Prepare:

1. Cut twelve small circles of construction paper to fit in the bottoms of the egg-carton cups.

2. With a bright marker, write the numbers 1–12 on the circles of paper.

3. Place the circles in the bottoms of the egg-carton cups, in order, as shown in the illustration.

☆ Activity:

Demonstrate, then have your child follow these steps:

1. Point to the number 1 in the bottom of the first cup. Say, "One." Take one cereal O and put it in the cup.

2. Point to the number 2 in the second cup and say, "Two." Count two cereal O's into the cup. Say, "One, two. Two."

3. Continue until all the cereal O's are placed in the cups. Point to each cup in turn and count from one to twelve. Return the cereal O's to the bowl and put the game away.

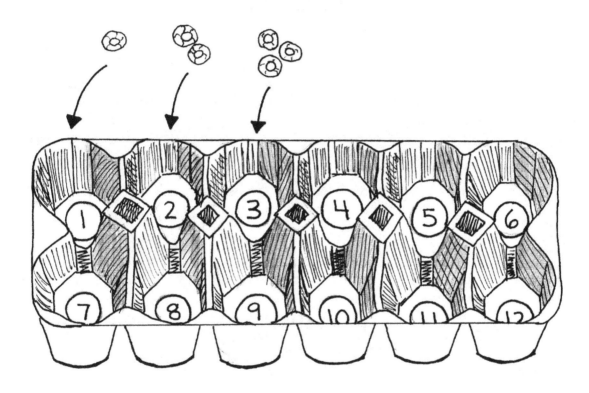

❧ 20 ❧

CHEERY CALENDAR

Visiting a personalized calendar each morning is a nice way to connect with your child and discuss the day's activities. Prepare the calendar in advance of a new month so you can begin the Activity on day 1. Decorate it with pictures that highlight seasons, study units, or special activities.

☞ **What You Need:**

Bowl of cereal O's, one sheet poster board, colored paper, colored markers, glue, scissors, ruler, small bowl, clear contact paper (optional)

✂ **To Prepare:**

1. Cut thirty-one 3¼- by 3½-inch rectangles of colored paper. Follow these steps with each piece to form the pockets:

   a. Fold in both the 3½-inch sides by ½ inch.

   b. Fold each flap in a second time, lengthwise, like an accordion, so the edges face out.

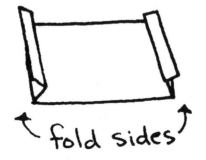

c. Fold over one of the short edges ¼ inch to create the bottom of the pocket.

← fold up bottom ↗

2. Write the numbers 1–31 on the fronts of the pockets.

3. Arrange the pockets on the poster board, as shown on page 65, and glue them into place, applying adhesive only the sides and bottom edges of each one.

4. (Optional) Apply clear contact paper over the upper section of the calendar so pictures and labels can be applied and removed without ripping the poster board.

5. Write the name of the month on a large rectangle of construction paper and tape it to the top of the calendar.

6. Attach the calendar to a wall or set it in a place where your child can reach it.

☆ **Activity:**

1. Set the bowl of cereal O's by the calendar. Place the small bowl (for counting the O's) beside it.

2. Introduce the calendar to your child and read the name of the month. Discuss special events such as birthdays, outings, or seasonal activities that will occur during the month. Talk about what kind of weather you might expect to have during this time.

3. Invite her to read the numbers on the pockets. Help if needed.

4. Recite the Months of the Year rhyme:

   > Thirty days hath September,
   > April, June, and November.
   > All the rest have thirty-one,
   > Except February which has twenty-eight.

   Ask her how many days the current month has.

5. Count one cereal O into the counting bowl. Say, "One." Count one again as you tuck the cereal O into the 1 pocket. Remove the cereal O from the pocket and have your child repeat the action herself. Explain that every day she will do this with the same number of O's as the date.

6. Invite her to decorate the calendar with seasonal art, her crafts and writings, or pictures. Each morning invite her to count into the bowl and pocket the same number of cereal O's that correspond to the date. Variation: Choose a theme for the month, such as horses, food, clothes, cars, tools, toys, things that make me happy, water, trees, numbers, or letters. Decorate the calendar and do projects on that subject.

Variation:

Choose a theme for the month, such as horses, food, clothes, cars, tools, toys, things that make me happy, water, trees, numbers, or letters. Decorate the calendar and do projects on that subject.

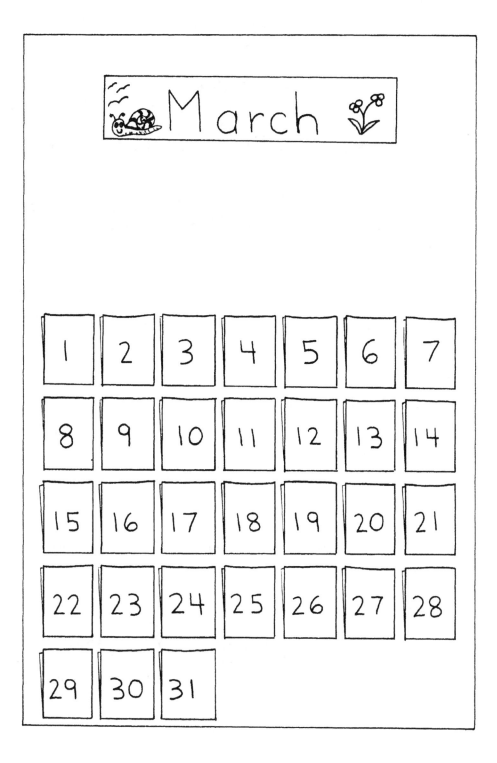

❧ 21 ❧

ADDING: PUTTING TOGETHER

All you need is a bowl of cereal O's to teach your child addition. He can clearly see the result of "putting together" two piles of little O's, which makes the abstract concept of addition real.

☞ What You Need:

Bowl of cereal O's, white paper, construction paper, colored markers, scissors, ruler, stapler, basket

✂ To Prepare:

1. Cut paper into 1- by 2½-inch slips.

2. Write simple addition problems (such as 4 + 4 =, 2 + 6 =, 9 + 1 =) on the slips, using the numbers 1–9.

3. Place the Addition Slips in the basket, making sure they are upside down.

☆ Activity:

1. Select one Addition Slip. Read the problem aloud, for example, "Three plus four equals."

2. Count out two piles of cereal O's. Three cereal O's in the first pile; four cereal O's in the second pile.

3. Explain that addition means "putting together." Sweep the two piles together and say, "Three plus four equals" . . . count the pile, "One, two, three, four, five, six, seven." Now say the whole problem, "Three plus four equals seven."

4. Put the cereal O's back in the bowl and set the Addition Slip aside. Invite your child to choose a new slip and repeat steps 1–3 himself.

Variation: Addition Books

After your child has worked some addition problems and understands the process, give him slips of paper to make his own addition book. Print the problems for a beginning writer so he only writes the answers. A child with more advanced skills can write the problems as well.

Have him follow these steps:

1. Copy the problem on a slip of paper (parent or child).

2. Find the solution with cereal O's.

3. Write the answer.

When ten slips are completed, cut a bright construction paper cover, staple the pages together at the side, and title it "My Addition Book." Have your child read you the booklet often to reinforce the lesson.

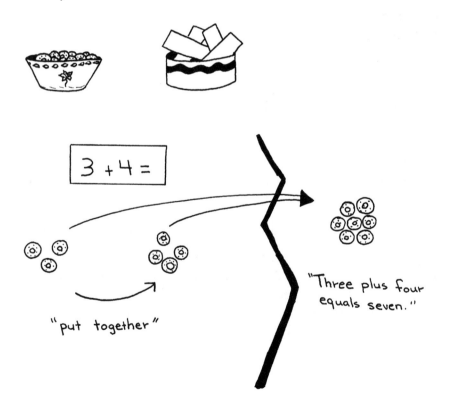

❧ 22 ❧

SUBTRACTING: TAKE IT AWAY!

When you subtract, you take something away from a group. The concept becomes clear with this fun activity.

☞ What You Need:

Bowl of cereal O's, white paper, construction paper, colored markers, scissors, ruler, stapler, basket

✄ To Prepare:

1. Cut paper into 1- by 2½-inch slips.

2. Write simple subtraction problems (such as 5 - 2 =, 8 - 7 =, and 10 - 3 =) on the slips, using the numbers 1–10.

3. Place the Subtraction Slips upside down in the basket.

☆ Activity:

1. Select one Subtraction Slip. Read the problem, for example, "Six minus two equals."

2. Count out one pile of cereal O's for the first number, in our example, six.

3. Explain that subtraction means "taking away." From the pile, count out the number of cereal O's for the second number, for example, two. Set the two cereal O's to the right of the big pile. Now dramatically scoop the two cereal O's up with your hand to "take them away." Redeposit them in the bowl or, to really make them disappear, eat them!

4. Count the remaining cereal O's to see how many are left. Say, "One, two, three, four." Now say the whole problem, "Six minus two equals four."

5. Put the cereal O's back in the bowl and set the Subtraction Slip aside. Invite your child to choose a new slip and repeat steps 1–4 herself.

Variation: Subtraction Books

After your child has worked some subtraction problems and understands the process, give her slips of paper to make her own subtraction book. Print the problems for a beginning writer so she only writes the answers. A child with more advanced skills can write the problems as well.

Have her follow these steps:

    1. Copy the problem on a slip of paper (parent or child).

    2. Find the solution with cereal O's.

    3. Write the answer.

When ten slips are completed, cut a bright construction paper cover, staple the pages together at the side, and title it "My Subtraction Book." Have her read you the booklet often to reinforce the lesson.

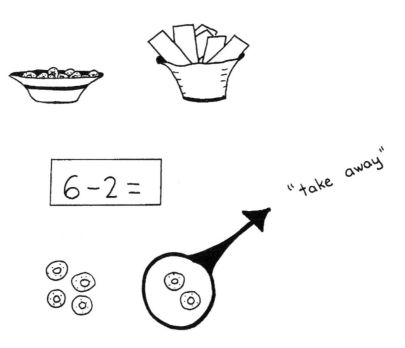

❧ 23 ❧

NUMBER SQUARES

Multiplication means adding a number to itself over and over again. These simple activities help your child understand the concept. Squared numbers—like 2 x 2, 3 x 3, and 4 x 4—create literal squares when displayed with cereal O's.

☞ **What You Need:**

Bowl of cereal O's, white paper, colored markers, scissors, ruler

✂ **To Prepare:**

1. Cut ten 1½- by 1½-inch squares of paper.

2. Write the numbers 1–10 (one number on each paper) to make Number Slips.

☆ **Activity 1:**

1. Explain that you are going to show how number squares are built.

2. Place the Number Slips 1, 2, and 3 on the table.

3. Place one cereal O's under number 1. Say, "One taken one time is one. One squared is one." Place two sets of cereal O's (as shown on page 71) under number 2 so they form a square. Count the cereal O's. Say, "Two taken two times is four. Two squared is four." Place three sets of three cereal O's under number 3 so they form a square. Count the cereal O's. Say, "Three taken three times is nine. Three squared is nine."

4. If your child shows interest, continue building squares while encouraging him to place the cereal O's and count. If his attention wanders, conclude the activity and return to it on another day.

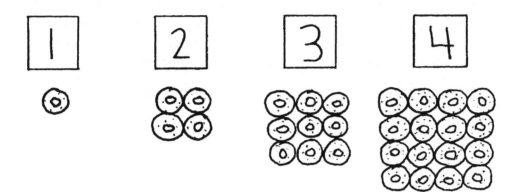

Variation:
Write numbers and equations on papers, as shown below. Have your child glue on the corresponding cereal O's.

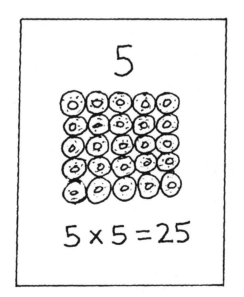

☆ **Activity 2:**

Write multiplication problems that are not squares (such as 2 x 5 =, 6 x 4 =, and 3 x 8 =) on slips of paper and have your child work them. Let's use 2 x 5 = for example. Ask him to read the problem and place two cereal O's beside the card. Say, "Two taken one time." Place a second set of two cereal O's beneath the first set. Say, "Two taken two times." Place a third set of two cereal O's and say, "Two taken three times." Place a fourth set of two cereal O's and say, "Two taken four times." Place the final set of two cereal O's and say, "Two taken five times equals" . . . count the cereal O's, "One, two, three, . . . ten." Now say the whole equation, "Two taken five times equals ten." Have him choose another problem and work it in similar manner.

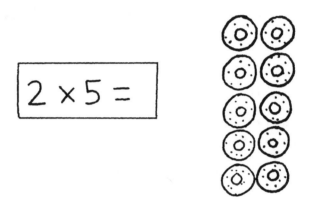

Variation: Multiplication Books

After your child has worked some multiplication problems and understands the process, give him slips of paper to make his own multiplication book.

Have him follow these steps:

1. Copy the problem on a slip of paper.

2. Find the solution with cereal O's.

3. Write the answer.

When ten slips are completed, cut a bright construction paper cover, staple the pages together at the side, and title it "My Multiplication Book." Have him read you the booklet often to reinforce the lesson. As an ongoing project, he could also make a book of ten pages for each number 1–10.

❧ 24 ❧

DIVISION PARTY

Division means finding how many times one quantity is contained in another. To simplify, we present the concept in terms your child can understand by dividing cereal O's among "friends" and explaining that division means sharing equally.

☞ **What You Need:**

Bowl of cereal O's, white paper, colored markers, scissors, basket, ten egg-carton cups or paper coffee-cup coasters

✄ **To Prepare:**

1. Write the names of friends and family on the egg-carton cups or coasters.

2. Cut the paper into 1- by 2½-inch slips

3. Write simple division problems (such as 15 ÷ 3 =, 24 ÷ 6 =, 8 ÷ 2 =, 9 ÷ 3 =, 4 ÷ 4 =, 16 ÷ 4 =, and 12 ÷ 2 =) on the slips.

4. Place the Division Slips upside down in the basket.

☆ **Activity:**

1. Explain that when we divide, we are sharing equally. Use a box of candy for example. Say, "If there were four people in your family and the box contained four pieces of candy, how many pieces would each person get? If there were eight pieces of candy, then how many would each person get? What if there were sixty-four pieces of candy? Not sure? That is why we have division. To help us divide equally."

2. Select one Division Slip and read the problem, "Twenty-one divided by seven equals." Explain that this means you have twenty-one items that need to be divided into seven equal parts. Another way to say it is that twenty-one cereal O's will be divided equally among seven people. Count out twenty-one cereal O's into a pile.

3. Set out seven egg-carton cups or paper coffee coasters to represent seven people. Put one cereal O in each cup or on each coaster. Now add a second round of cereal O's. Distribute seven cereal O's a third time. All the cereal O's are now divided equally.

4. Ask your child to count how many cereal O's each person received. Conclude by saying, "Twenty-one divided by seven equals three. Each person got three cereal O's."

5. Put the cereal O's back in the bowl and set the division problem aside. Invite her to choose a new Division Slip and repeat steps 2–4 herself.

Variation: Division Books
After your child has worked some equations and understands the process, give her slips of paper to make her own book.

Have her follow these steps:
1. Copy the problem on a slip of paper.

2. Find the solution with cereal O's.

3. Write the answer.

When ten slips are completed, cut a bright construction paper cover, staple the pages together at the side, and write "My Division Book" on the cover. Have her read you the book often to reinforce the lesson.

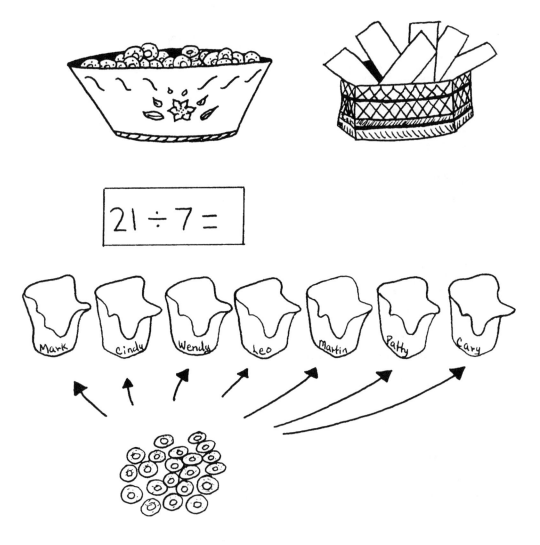

$21 \div 7 =$

✌ 25 ✌

COUNT TO 100

This clear, dramatic presentation helps your child understand the quantity one hundred and the relationship of the numbers to each other.

☞ What You Need:

Bowl of cereal O's, two contrasting 8½- by 11-inch pieces of construction paper, colored markers, white glue, ruler, scissors

✄ To Prepare:

1. Draw ten lines, ¾ inch apart, lengthwise on one sheet of construction paper. Cut off the excess paper along the tenth line.

2. Draw ten lines, 1 inch apart, across the width of the paper. Cut off the excess paper. Your chart should now measure 7½ by 10 inches.

3. Write the numbers 1–100 in the lower part of the boxes, as shown in the illustration. (Optional: Write each line of numbers with a different colored marker.) Leave space for a cereal O to be glued above each number.

   Note: An older child can write the numbers himself.

4. Glue the chart onto the second piece of construction paper. Choose a contrasting color to give it a nice border.

☆ Activity 1:

Demonstrate, then ask your child to say each number and glue a cereal O into the box. Work in order from 1–100. Some children will finish the project in one sitting. Others may prefer doing one line daily.

☆ **Activity 2:**

Demonstrate, then ask your child to say each number and glue a cereal O into the box. Work in order from 1–100. Some children will finish the project in one sitting. Others may prefer doing one line daily.

☆ **Activity 3:**

Show your child how to count by tens as he points to the numbers. Say, "Ten, twenty, thirty, . .. one hundred!"

1	2	3	4	5	6	7	8	9	10
11	12	13	14	15	16	17	18	19	20
21	22	23	24	25	26	27	28	29	30
31	32	33	34	35	36	37	38	39	40
41	42	43	44	45	46	47	48	49	50
51	52	53	54	55	56	57	58	59	60
61	62	63	64	65	66	67	68	69	70
71	72	73	74	75	76	77	78	79	80
81	82	83	84	85	86	87	88	89	90
91	92	93	94	95	96	97	98	99	100

✦ 26 ✦

TENS NECKLACE

In addition to being fun, stringing cereal O's focuses concentration and improves coordination. Invite your child to count the O's as she strings them.

☞ **What You Need:**

Bowl of cereal O's, beads or tubular pasta, thick thread (string or yarn), blunt craft needle

☆ **Activity:**

1. With your child, measure a length of thread (string or yarn) 4 inches longer than the necklace she wants. Make sure it is long enough to slip over her head comfortably.

2. Thread the needle.

3. Pass the needle and thread through one cereal O and tie it in place. Leave a 2-inch tail at the end.

4. Have her string cereal O's, counting each one until there are 10. Now add a bead or piece of tubular pasta as a marker. Continue in like fashion until a 2-inch tail remains.

5. Remove the needle and tie the ends together. Count round the necklace by tens. Compliment your child on her beautiful Cereal O's Necklace and invite her to wear it.

Variation 1: Bracelet
Make a matching bracelet.

Variation 2: Add Variety

Substitute tubular pasta or large beads for some or all of the cereal O's, letting your child's creativity guide the design. Suggest she decorate the pasta with colored markers for more color.

Variation 3: Doubling Necklace

Invite your child to make a special necklace with you. The goal is to string plain cereal O's in a doubling pattern, separated by either a colorful bead or three colored cereal O's.

Working together, tie one cereal O two inches from the end of the yarn. This is "one." Next, string a colored bead or three colored cereal O's, which act as dividers. Add two plain O's. String the bead or colored O's dividers. Continue doubling the plain cereal O's—four, eight, sixteen—each time alternating with a bead or three colored O. For the middle of the necklace, string thirty-two O's. Again add a bead or colored O's. Continue adding O's and dividers in decreasing order: sixteen, eight, four, two, and one. Tie the ends together. Suggest your child wear the necklace and share its secret (by reciting its doubling numbers) with friends.

Variation 4: Feed the Birds Necklace

String popcorn, raisins, or fresh or dried cranberries with the cereal O's. The needle and thread will get quite sticky, but the project is still fun. After your child wears it a while, have him hang it on a tree for some hungry birds.

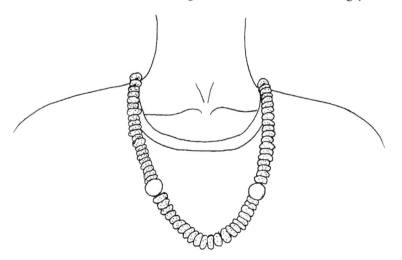

✌ 27 ✌

GUESS HOW MANY

This project helps your child learn to estimate and to make a simple chart. And it gives him the opportunity to practice social skills while interacting with friends, neighbors, and family. Remind him to say please when asking for guesses and to thank people for their help.

☞ **What You Need:**

Box of cereal O's, jar with lid, paper, pencil

☆ **Activity 1:**

1. Ask your child to pour cereal O's into the jar and secure the lid.

2. Tell him to observe the jar closely, estimate how many cereal O's are in it, then write his name and guess on a sheet of paper.

3. Have him show the jar to neighbors, friends, or other family members, asking each person to write his or her name and guess on the paper.

4. Invite him to pour out the cereal O's and count them with you. Then put the cereal back into the jar and give it to the person whose guess was closest to the correct number.

☆ **Activity 2:**

1. Gather a group of friends or family members.

2. Ask each person to estimate how many cereal O's they can hold in one hand. Write their names and guesses on a piece of paper.

3. Have each person grab a big handful of O's from a box of cereal and place it in a separate pile on a table. Invite your child to count the O's in the piles and write the number next to each guess. Whose prediction came closest?

Variation:
Create a bar graph, illustrated below, using the information gathered.

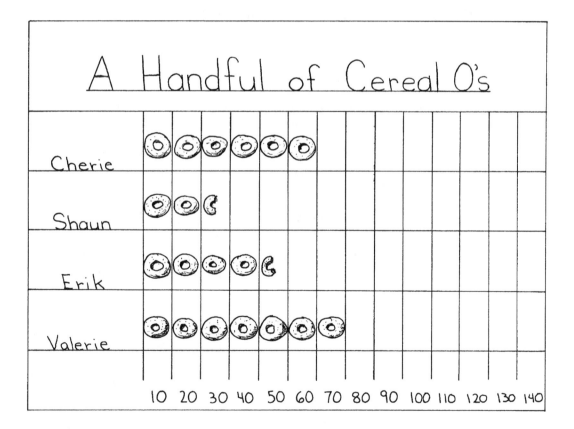

BUILD-A-SHAPE

Building with marshmallows, cereal O's, and toothpicks allows your child to experiment with geometric figures. She will discover how lines and points define shapes, and then explore two- and three-dimensional figures.

☞ **What You Need:**

Cereal O's, miniature marshmallows, toothpicks with points at both ends, paper, pencil

☆ **Activity 1:**

1. Show your child a marshmallow. Say, "This is a point. Yes, it's a marshmallow, but for now we'll call it a point. A point means stop."

2. Show a toothpick. Say, "This is a line. Yes, it's a toothpick, but for now we'll call it a line. See the sharp ends? They tell us to think this line goes on forever in both directions."

3. Have her put a marshmallow on one end of the toothpick, then string cereal O's on the toothpick and put a marshmallow on the second end. Say, "The marshmallow points tell us the line stops. The line doesn't go on forever anymore. We have captured a piece of the line. We call this a line segment."

4. Invite her to build her own line segments.

5. Draw a line segment on paper. Have your child trace it and draw more of her own.

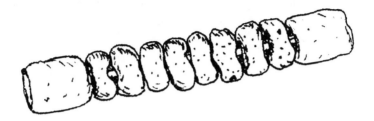

☆ **Activity 2:**

1. On another day, bring out the cereal O's, marshmallows, and toothpicks. Review the terms point, line, and line segment.

2. Demonstrate how to build a triangle with three line segments.

3. Encourage her to build lots of triangles.

4. Draw a triangle on paper. Have her trace it and draw more of her own.

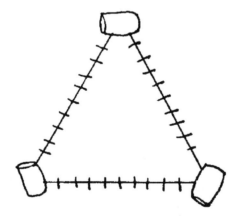

☆ **Activity 3:**

When she is ready, show her how to build additional shapes, such as squares, rectangles, pentagons, hexagons, heptagons, and octagons (four-, five-, six-, seven-, and eight-sided shapes respectively).

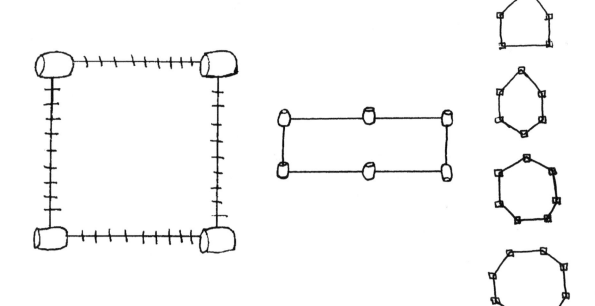

☆ **Activity 4:**

Try building three-dimensional forms such as cubes, pyramids, and rectangular prisms.

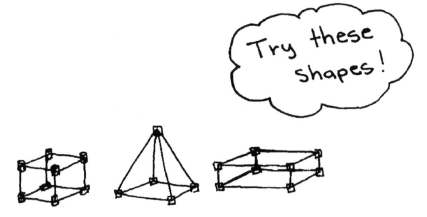

Try these shapes!

❧ 29 ❧

SEWING SHAPES

Simple up-and-down stitches attach cereal O's to fabric in this dual-purpose activity that helps your child becomes familiar with geometric shapes while developing his coordination skills.

☞ **What You Need:**

Bowl of cereal O's, large blunt sewing needle, fabric with a loose weave such as burlap or worn flannel, colored card stock or poster board, glue, thin yarn, dark-colored marker, ruler, scissors or box cutter

Caution: Only adults should handle a box cutter or other sharp blade.

✂ **To Prepare:**

1. Cut fabric into a 5½- by 6-inch rectangle.

2. Cut the card stock or poster board into two 6- by 6½-inch rectangles. Carefully cut a 5- by 5½-inch opening into one of the rectangles with scissors or a box cutter to create a ½-inch frame.

3. Draw a vertical line on the fabric and write the word line at the bottom with the marker.

4. Thread the needle with yarn and tie a knot at the end.

☆ **Activity 1:**

1. Beginning at one end of the line, sew one cereal O onto the fabric. Invite your child to add cereal O's by stitching up and down over the O's and through the fabric. Secure the end by looping under another stitch and tying a knot. (To make this activity easier, glue the cereal O's in place before sewing.)

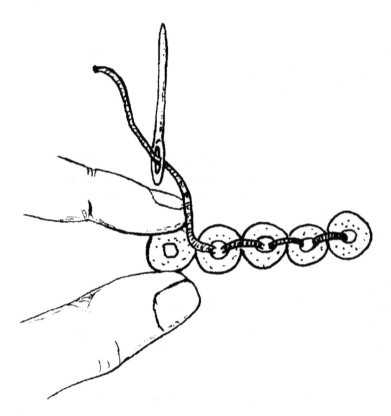

2. Glue the fabric onto the solid piece of card stock or poster board.

3. Place the frame over the picture and glue in place.

4. Press the edges and let dry.

5. Hang or set the finished project where your child can see it.

Variation:

Repeat the above steps to create a triangle, square, and circle. Heighten interest by doing a different shape each day.

☆ **Activity 2:**

1. Show your child how to trace the shapes with his fingers and say their names.

2. Encourage him to find objects in your home that have the same shapes.

✌ SCIENCE ✌

The lessons that follow give your child a taste of science, help her catch the spirit of exploration, and teach her how to set up an experiment so she can find answers for herself. In this short section we touch on the following topics:

Goal 1: Learn how to set up an experiment, run tests, and collect data
> Lessons 30–32 introduce your child to the scientific method with fun, hands-on activities.

Goal 2: Learn to arrange data on a chart
> Lessons 30–32 offer practice organizing and presenting facts acquired from experimentation.

Goal 3: Find out about the planets in our solar system
> Lesson 33 teaches your child how to research a topic and build a model based on information she has gathered.

Goal 4: Investigate a property of physics
> Lesson 34 helps her discover the properties of a lever.

Let your child's curiosity guide your science study. When she asks why the sky is blue, how come unsweetened chocolate is bitter, why apples turn brown, what fingernails are made of, why ice melts, etc., use these questions as opportunities to teach her how to find the answers in books, online, or through experimentation.

✧ 30 ✧

BALANCE SCALE

In this lesson, your child uses a homemade balance scale to weigh things. She then learns to arrange her findings on a graph.

☞ **What You Need:**

Bowl of cereal O's, two small paper cups, scissors, ruler, wooden spoon, book, wooden skewer, paper, pencil, string, white glue, assorted small items (such as a penny, paper clip, button, or dime)

✂ **To Prepare:**

1. Use scissors (or a sharp knife) to cut the pointed end off the skewer.

2. Cut one 12-inch and two 18-inch lengths of string.

3. Tie the middle of the string around the center of the skewer. Now knot the two ends of the string to make a loop (see illustration, page 90).

4. Use a sharp pencil to punch two holes in opposite sides of each cup.

5. Thread one 18-inch length of string through the holes in a cup, then loop both ends of the string around one end of the skewer and tie a double knot. Repeat with other cup and string on the other end of the skewer.

6. Place a wooden spoon so the handle extends off the edge of a table. Secure the other end of the spoon with a book. Hang the balance on the handle, as shown.

7. Adjust the knotted strings that hold the cups so they balance. Attach the knots to the skewer with a drop of white glue. Let dry.

☆ Activity 1:

1. Show your child that the cups are level. The scale is balanced.

2. Have her place cereal O's one at a time into the left hand cup. Notice that as the weight in the cup increases, gravity pulls it lower.

3. One by one, have her add cereal O's to the right hand cup until it balances. Did it take the same number of cereal O's? Why or why not?

☆ Activity 2:

Invite your child to use the balance scale to weigh other light objects, such as a dime, button, paper clip, plastic spoon, ring, or a flower. Write down how many cereal O's it takes to balance each one.

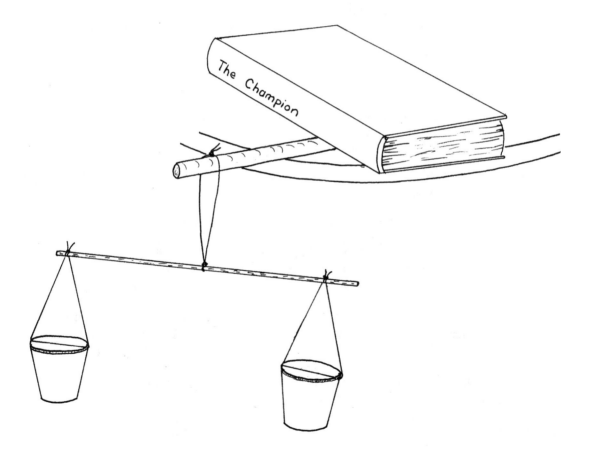

☆ **Activity 3:**

Use the information gathered in Activity 2 to make a bar graph with your child, as shown below.

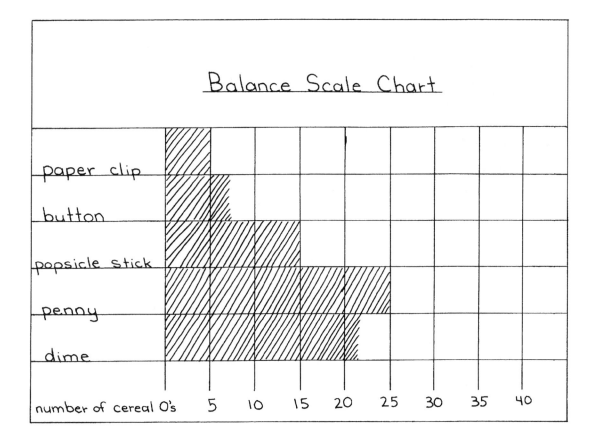

৯ 31 ৯

INSECT TASTE TEST

Don't worry, I'm not asking your child to eat insects! Instead, this activity helps him discover what insects like to eat. It encourages keen observation and guides him to organize his findings on a chart.

☞ **What You Need:**

Cereal O's, shoebox-sized box, insects (try ants, beetles, or earwigs), small pieces of meat, fruit, and lettuce

☆ **Activity 1:**

1. Have your child place cereal O's, meat, fruit, and lettuce separately in the four corners of the box.

2. Help him gently place an insect in the center of the box. Watch which food it prefers and make a written note of what it eats. This may take a while, so be patient.

3. Ask him to carefully return the insect to its home and then find a different one and repeat the test.

☆ Activity 2:

Assist your child in using the information he gathered in Activity 1 to make a bar graph of his own, as shown below.

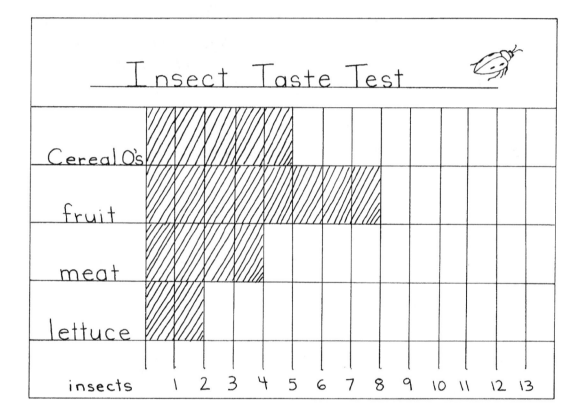

‿ 32 ‿

MY WEATHER CHART

Introduce the process of observation and notation by taking a few minutes each day to look at the weather with your child. Show her how to record the findings on a chart and then check the weather in the local media. Are the reports similar?

☞ **What You Need:**

Bowl of cereal O's, 8½- by 11-inch construction paper, colored markers, ruler, white glue

✂ **To Prepare:**

1. Draw nine horizontal lines, ¾ inch apart, lengthwise on a sheet of construction paper. Measure and draw the nine lines from the bottom up. Write "My Weather Chart" above the top line, as shown on page 95.

2. Beneath the top line, draw seven vertical lines, 1¼ inches apart, measuring from the right short edge and moving left.

3. Complete the chart, referring to the illustration, by adding the words and symbols for sunny, partly cloudy, cloudy, foggy, windy, rainy, stormy, and snowy weather.

4. Write the days of the week at the bottom.

5. Tape the chart to the wall or refrigerator, or keep it in a handy place for the Activity.

Note: To make charts for several children or for more than one week, photocopy your original design onto colored paper.

☆ **Activity:**

1. Explain to your child that she is going to watch the weather every day and keep a record of it for a week. Look at the chart together and explain what the symbols mean. Point out the days of the week at the bottom of the chart. Practice saying their names.

2. Ask her to check the weather daily and tell you what she notices. Invite her to glue cereal O's onto the spaces that match her observations.

3. At the week's end, review the chart and discuss the weather pattern together. Is it usual for this time of year?

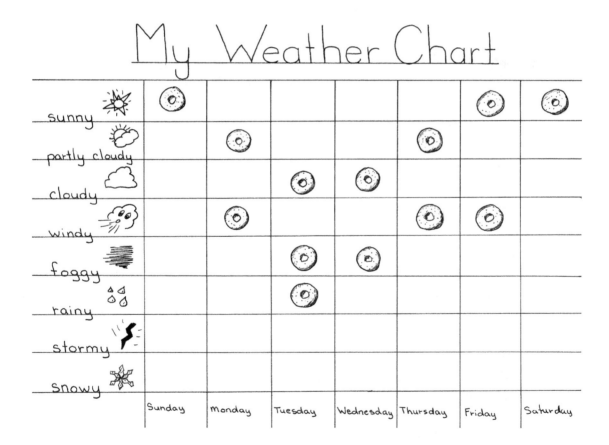

❧ 33 ❧

OUR SOLAR SYSTEM

This activity is a great way to introduce the solar system and Earth's place among the planets. Before you do the project, visit the library with your child and check out books on the subject. Also look at photos of the planets on the internet. Together, study one planet at a time and then add it to the solar system chart.

☞ What You Need:

Bowl of cereal O's, white and colored 8½- by 11-inch construction paper, white glue, colored markers, ruler, scissors, plastic bag, rolling pin or can, information about the solar system (library books and internet).

✀ To Prepare:

1. Glue twelve sheets of white paper together (three across and four down), overlapping the edges ¼ inch. Let dry.

2. Draw a 5-inch diameter orange circle in the center of the paper. (Sketch the circle freehand; don't worry about drawing it perfectly.) This represents the orbit of Mercury. Working outward from the orange line, draw concentric circles 1½ inches apart on the paper in this order:

   a. Venus–pink
   b. Earth–green
   c. Mars–red
   d. Asteroid Belt–pencil or light grey
   e. Jupiter–yellow
   f. Saturn–brown
   g. Uranus–purple
   h. Neptune–blue
   i. Pluto–black

☆ **Activity 1:**

1. Invite your child to draw the Sun in the center of the paper. Explain that the Sun is a fiery, hot star. We feel the energy from it as warmth and light. Without it no plants or animals could live on Earth, which would be dark and very cold. Tell him that there are eight planets in our solar system—plus Pluto (a dwarf planet)—and that we live on the one called Earth. The planets circle the Sun. It takes Earth one year to travel around the Sun. Ask him how many times Earth has circled the Sun during his life. Look at books about the solar system.

2. Make the planets (page 99) with your child by gluing cereal O's on circles of paper that match the colors of their orbits. Larger planets use more cereal O's to indicate their relative size. Let dry before proceeding.

Mercury–orange	1 cereal O
Venus–pink	4 cereal O's
Earth–green	4 cereal O's
Mars–red	1 cereal O
Jupiter–yellow	19 cereal O's
Saturn–brown	19 cereal O's
Uranus–purple	7 cereal O's
Neptune–blue	7 cereal O's
Pluto–black	1 cereal O

Note: To make Uranus and Neptune, glue one cereal O on the paper, then add a ring of six O's around it. To make Jupiter and Saturn, glue one O on the paper, add a ring of six O's around it, then finally glue on a second ring of twelve O's.

3. Pick up Mercury. Say, "This is Mercury, the planet closest to the Sun." Ask your child to move Mercury around the Sun on the orange line to show its orbit, then glue it into place anywhere along the line.

4. Repeat for Venus, Earth, and Mars.

5. Explain that the asteroid belt is a huge ring of rocks and dust that circle the Sun between Mars and Jupiter. To make the asteroid belt, crush cereal O's in a plastic bag with a rolling pin or can. Spread a ½-inch-wide layer of glue on the grey line and have him sprinkle on the crushed cereal. Let set for a few minutes, then shake off the excess crumbs.

6. Continue gluing the remaining planets as before. Draw a dotted line around Saturn with yellow marker to represent the rings.

☆ **Activity 2:**

1. Cut nine 1- by 3-inch labels from white paper.

2. Write, or have your child write, the name of each planet (and its astronomical symbol–optional) with the color that matches its orbit.

3. Have him glue the labels next to the planets.

Mercury ☿
Venus ♀
Earth ⊕
Mars ♂
Jupiter ♃
Saturn ♄
Uranus ♅
Neptune ♆
Pluto ♇

☆ **Activity 3:**

Look at the Solar System Chart together and have him say the names of the planets in order from the Sun outward. Ask him to tell you what he found most interesting during his study. Invite him to choose a planet and imagine would it be like to visit it. Would he want to? Why or why not?

Variation:
Have an older child draw a picture of each planet on separate half- or full-sheets of paper and write a descriptive sentence or paragraph for each one. Add a construction paper cover and staple the pages at the side to make a Solar System Book.

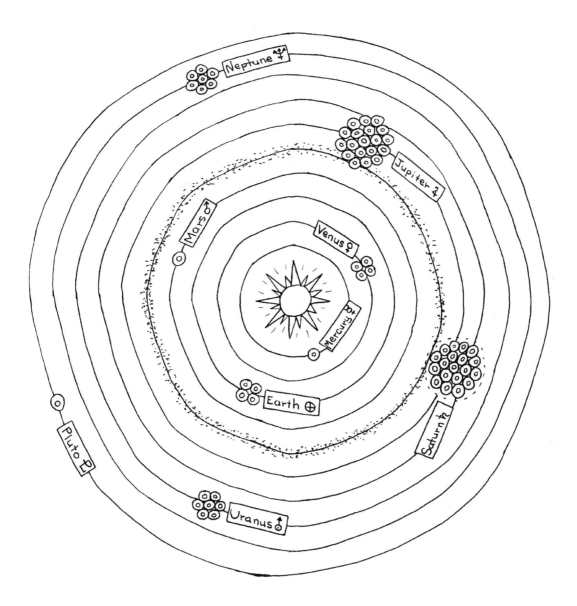

✧ 34 ✧

JUMPING CEREAL O'S

This activity demonstrates the properties of a lever. It is great fun, but because it leaves cereal O's scattered around the floor, have your child pick up each one as it "jumps" or have a "search party" gather them when the game is finished. Add math practice by measuring and noting the distance of each jump.

Caution: To keep your Jumping Cereal O's activity safe, make sure everyone is behind the launch site so they don't get hit by airborne cereal.

☞ What You Need:
Bowl of cereal O's, wooden spoon, popsicle stick, chopstick (optional)

☆ Activity 1:
Demonstrate, then have your child follow these steps:

1. Set the wooden spoon horizontally in front of you.

2. Lay the popsicle stick across the spoon so that 1 inch extends over the handle, away from you (see illustration).

3. Place a cereal O on the popsicle-stick end nearest you.

4. Quickly press the far end of the stick to the table and watch the cereal O jump away!

☆ **Activity 2:**

Jumping Cereal O's illustrates the action of a lever. This activity introduces two new words to describe this simple machine.

1. Explain that the popsicle stick is a lever. The point where it meets the spoon is called the fulcrum. Invite your child to experiment by changing the position of the fulcrum. What happens when the O's jump?

2. Change the length of the lever by having her use a chopstick instead of a popsicle stick. What happens?

3. Invite her to look for other levers such as a crowbar, simple can opener, teetertotter, wheelbarrow, or shovel. Discuss how they make work easier.

Variation 1:

Invite her to place several cereal O's on the end of the lever and make them jump together.

Variation 2:

String a piece of yarn across two chairs. Invite her to jump the cereal O's over the yarn.

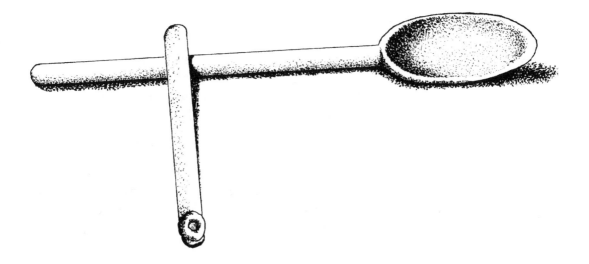

∽ TIPS FOR PARENTING ∽

Dear parents and caregivers,

You have been entrusted with a life. A human life. And you have the opportunity to introduce this child to the world with all its marvels. Her experiences, her experiments, her environment, all provide elements with which she builds her future self—the adult she will become.

The first three years are remarkable. With no formal instruction your child will learn to walk and talk, develop a strong sense of self, and figure out how to interact with the world. Your home is her classroom and you are her first teacher.

Look at your house from your child's perspective: get down on your hands and knees so you are at her eye level. What do you see? Is the environment clean and hazard free? Does she have a place for her things? Are there any wall decorations set at her level? Here are some ideas to make your home child friendly and to help her become more self-sufficient:

- Eliminate clutter. Sort through her things, including clothing, and discard those that are no longer needed. Make a "home" for the remaining items so they can be stored neatly when not in use. Low shelves, which can be set up with bricks and boards, are great for storing toys and books. Plastic bins or cardboard boxes (made attractive with a coating of decorative contact paper) set on edge also work well for organizing stuff.

- Beautify: Place pretty pictures at her eye level. Add a small plant or a vase of flowers.

- Encourage work: Provide a space, even if it is part of a table, that is her own. If possible, give her a child-sized chair and table for her projects. Collect markers, crayons, colored pencils, paper, glue, scissors, etc. in her area to promote creative exploration.

- Encourage reading: Assemble a comfy area—a small chair, beanbag chair, or a few pillows thrown in a corner—with a collection of books nearby.

- Help her be independent:

  - ✛ Set a stool in front of the bathroom sink so she can wash her hands by herself.

  - ✛ Keep a cup and pitcher of water in a place where she can reach them and serve herself when she is thirsty.

  - ✛ Put small cleaning cloths in a convenient basket so she can clean up accidental spills.

Invite your child to join you as you work around the house and encourage her attempts at independent action. Be tolerant of her failures and praise her successes. Give her little tasks that contribute to the family. When you fold clothes, for example, show her how to match socks and fold them together. Invite her to scribble on paper when you are writing or typing. And ask her to join you in preparing a meal by stirring batter, kneading a bit of dough, tearing lettuce, or cutting bananas with a plastic knife. She loves to do things for herself, so show her how!

Here are more activities to help her improve coordination, refine her senses, and learn new things:

- Sort items such as leaves, shells, nuts, fruit, shaped pasta, colored cotton balls, cereal, or candy into like piles.

- Polish copper, silver, or mirrors. (Make sure to supervise carefully.)

- Wash plant leaves.

- Draw pictures.

- Cut paper.

- Fold napkins and clothes.

- Wash toys, doll clothes, or a small chair or table.

- Match pairs of fruit, pictures, colors, numbers, or letters.

- Build a tower with plastic containers.

- Fill glasses with different amounts of water, then tap them gently with a spoon to hear the different sounds.

- Point out squares, circles, or triangles around your home and town.

- Find things that are the same color.

- Count sets of household items: pictures, faucets, rugs, forks, cups, etc.

- Find objects with names that begin with a chosen letter.

- Place word labels by corresponding items around the house.

- Plant seeds and watch them grow.

- Fill measuring cups with water and pour into each other to discover their relationship.

- Play with small movable objects to learn the basics of addition, subtraction, multiplication, and division.

The early years of childrearing can be challenging, but they are very important. The patterns you establish during this time form the foundation of your relationship with your child, one hopefully based on mutual respect, trust, and honest two-way communication.

You are her most influential teacher. She watches your every move with awe and copies your actions and speech, viewing you as an all-powerful being who makes her wishes come true and punishes her transgressions. With this in mind, try to see yourself through your child's eyes. How does she interact with you? Does she seem loving, timid, fearful, happy, secure, confident? Are there ways you can improve your relationship?

If you build the habit of truthfulness and trust with your child when she is young, she will have confidence to confide in you when she is a teenager. One way to engender trust is to let her know that she can tell you anything. Congratulate her when she tells you a difficult thing and let any discipline be tempered by the fact that she trusted you enough to tell the truth. Explain that we all make mistakes—nobody is perfect—and that when we do something that hurts another person, we must apologize and try to make amends. Tell her that you hope she makes good choices but no matter what she does, you will always love her.

Your child learns how to deal with difficult situations by watching you. When the inevitable trials of life cause you to lose your temper or make a poor decision—or if you are unable to fulfill a promise—give her a hug and tell her that you are sorry. Once an apology is offered and forgiveness given, both parties can put the incident aside and move forward without guilt or carrying a grudge. These life lessons give her the tools to interact with others with compassion and empathy. She learns that apologizing is a graceful way to deal with mistakes, and that by forgiving others, she can smooth awkward circumstances.

While honesty is important among family members, frank speech in public can produce embarrassing results. Your child has not been in the world very long, so don't assume that she knows how to use good manners. It is your job to teach her how to act and speak respectfully. Be patient and kind, but insist she stop rude behavior and replace it with appropriate actions. Teach her how to ask for things politely: "May I please have a glass of juice." Don't give her the juice until she puts the please in the sentence. Expect to hear thank you when you hand her the glass. Teaching this is simple. If you don't hear "the magic words," don't let go of the glass.

So what do you do if your child begins speaking rudely to you? When my son, Christopher, was a toddler, he suddenly developed the habit of saying "No Way!" when asked to do something. My husband and I taught him to say "Yes, Mommy!" or "Yes, Daddy!" instead. We insisted that he give the proper response. He soon learned that all activity stopped until he answered properly. He was free to express a complaint and knew that he could discuss things with us, but when we gave him a direct order, we expected him to obey. We knew that obedience was important for his safety, for if Christopher were about to run into the street in front of a car and we told him to stop, he must obey.

Childhood should be a time of exploration, learning, and delight, so limit rules to important things. But stand firm on points that matter. Expect your child to obey a command, tell the truth, be kind to animals and people, and be gentle with objects so they don't break. Within these boundaries, give her freedom to make her own choices and be creative.

She learns by doing, so allow her to take small risks. Let her try to carry a glass of water into the next room. If it spills, she gets a cloth and wipes up the puddle. If she drops the glass and it breaks, it is no great loss, but she learns to be more careful next time. She also learns from your reaction to the shattered glass. If you lose your temper, she may become fearful or angry and be less willing to take another chance.

If you stay calm and express sorrow at the loss, she will feel sad too. Have her bring you the dust pan and watch as you sweep up the shards. She will think about what happened while she watches you clean and make a greater effort next time. If she successfully carries the glass of water, watch the glow of satisfaction shine from her eyes. Yes, you could have carried it for her, but doing so would have denied her a little victory.

When faced with a decision about whether to intervene in your child's activity, ask yourself these questions: Will this matter in a year? Ten years? Will it affect her health or the development of her character? If it is reasonable, why not let her do or get what she wants? It may give her a burst of joy. Sometimes she will get a flash of inspiration for a project that you know will make a mess or is doomed to fail. If possible, let her do it. What she learns from the experience will make a greater impression than a few words from you.

Like most siblings, our children argued when they were young. They didn't have the skills to peacefully resolve some of their conflicts, so they came to us—each hoping to get his or her way. When this happened, we took time to listen to our son and daughter describe the situation from their respective viewpoints. Sometimes we were amazed to find that, using each child's logic, they were both right! A compromise had to be reached. If the children wouldn't budge, Mommy or Daddy had to act as judge and make a decision. We first encouraged them to find an agreement that made both happy. If that failed, we told them "the judge" would make a decision and there would be no argument about it. Then we ruled as fairly as possible, told them the reasons why we made the decision, and allowed no further discussion. Usually one or both children were unhappy, but with the verdict passed, life soon returned to normal.

I remember spending happy hours with my children, doing many of the projects listed in this book. As they played with Mom and Dad, they didn't know they were "in school." Instead they experienced the thrill of learning new things, which was deeply satisfying and rewarding.

In contrast, many youngsters spend countless hours staring at a screen. This robs them of time better spent in creative play, learning new skills, interacting with people, and being involved with activities that help them feel useful.

Young children cannot clearly distinguish between reality and fantasy—what they see makes a deep impression, influencing their character development and behavior—so take care what they view. When used as educational tools, television, electronic devices, and the internet can be windows to the world, showing a vast array of plants, animals, places, people, events, and ideas. So use them as a resource by scheduling viewing time carefully and then turning them off.

The early years are precious. One of the most important things you can teach your child is the ability to educate herself, which will allow her to pursue her passions with confidence. Help her learn this skill by promoting her innate curiosity and encouraging her to find ways to answer her own questions in books, on the internet, through experimentation, or by asking experts.

Whatever your circumstances, you can show your child the wonders of the world in little things around you. Make her life a marvelous adventure filled with new discoveries and wrap her in the security of your love. Take time to read to her daily. Your attention is more important to her than anything money can buy. Try to fill her hours with beautiful music, kind words, and moments of peace when she can watch the stars, ants at work, a spider spinning its web, or the clouds changing shapes. Even though she will not consciously remember much from these years, her experiences influence her character and shape her outlook on life.

I hope these ideas kindle the joy of learning for you and your loved ones. And I invite you to continue your *Play and Learn* adventure with *Read, Write, & Spell*, which offers a step-by-step guide to language instruction from preschool through grade three.

All my best,

Talita Paolini

❧ Acknowledgments ❧

When I was a young mother, I sold health products door to door for a time, trying to make a few extra bucks. One day I found myself in a dingy apartment, talking with a young, single mom. Her baby lay on a blanket spread out on the floor by her side. There were few furnishings. Her outlook was bleak. That night and for many nights to come, I thought of her. And I wondered . . . with her meager resources and limited education, how could she give her child a head start on learning? What, I wondered, was inexpensive and available everywhere? And that's when I thought of cereal! I don't know what happened to that woman and her now-grown child, but I hope they found their way to a better future. Unbeknownst to them, they were the inspiration for this book.

Fortunately, my background gave me the tools to transform that spark of an idea into this guidebook. But it wouldn't have happened without several people who profoundly influenced my life and helped me understand the nature of childhood: My mother, Barbara, who, though she was only with me during my early years, introduced me to the magic, wonder, and love of nature. And my teachers in the Montessori method, Dr. Elizabeth Caspari and Ellen Goodman, whose explanations of early childhood psychology and demonstrations of educational techniques gave me the foundation upon which I developed these lessons.

This second edition of *Play and Learn with Cereal O's* has been freshly edited and includes new lessons. I'm grateful to Immanuela Meijer, whose eye for detail was invaluable in clarifying the instructions and smoothing the text.

Most exciting of all is the fun new cover design, thanks to the wonderful Tara Mayberry!

Each book I write involves my entire family. Christopher, thanks for helping with the illustrations. Angela, your creative ideas are always an inspiration: Frame It!, Tower Power, Insect Taste Test, Our Solar System, and Jumping Cereal O's reflect your style. Kenneth, computer whiz and my love . . . thank you.

Teach with confidence and spark your child's joy of learning with these Paolini Method books!

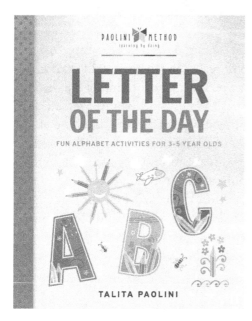

LETTER of the Day
Fun Alphabet Activities for 3–5 year olds

Tap into your child's curiosity with activities that introduce the alphabet through crafts and playful exploration of the environment. With 104 lessons to choose from, it's easy to find ones that spark excitement. Just pick a letter, do the project, and soon your little one will be pointing out letters everywhere and scribbling them for fun!

- Learn letter sounds and shapes

- Begin to write the alphabet

- Improve coordination

- Build concentration skills

- Discover how to find answers to questions

- Become more aware of their surroundings

Letter of the Day
Talita Paolini
228 pages, softcover
ISBN: 9780966621365

Order from paolinimethod.com or any bookstore.

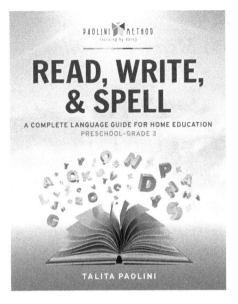

Read, Write, & Spell
A Complete Language Guide for Home Education Preschool–Grade 3

Read, Write, & Spell is your complete guide to teaching language skills at home. Inside you'll find a collection of hands-on activities to help children discover the joys of reading and writing, one step at a time. The lessons first establish a solid understanding of phonics and then build vocabulary skills through creative writing. Bite-sized tasks make it easy for students to complete each activity and feel a sense of victory as they progress.

- Identify the alphabet letters by sight and sound

- Read and write words, sentences, and short stories

- Create unique booklets of creative writing projects

- Develop beautiful cursive writing and expand vocabulary with a spelling notebook

- Organize information in book reports, reports on places, and biographies

- Build a grammar rainbow, learn the parts of speech . . . and more!

Read, Write, & Spell empowers you to teach your children with confidence and sets the stage for a lifelong love of learning!

Read, Write, & Spell
Talita Paolini
340 pages, softcover
ISBN: 0-9666213-4-4

Order from paolinimethod.com or any bookstore.

CPSIA information can be obtained
at www.ICGtesting.com
Printed in the USA
LVHW062319110319
610318LV00005B/66/P

9 780966 621372

❧ STAY IN TOUCH ❧

I hope you and your child spend many happy hours learning together with *Play and Learn with Cereal O's.* Please share your stories and photos on social media, using #PaoliniMethod, so others can be inspired by your projects!

Twitter: twitter.com/paolinimethod
Facebook: facebook.com/paolinimethod
Instagram: instagram.com/paolinimethod
Pinterest: pinterest/paolinimethod

And come visit my website, PaoliniMethod.com, where you'll discover more fun educational activities!

❧ HELP A CHILD TODAY ❧

The simple, powerful activities contained in *Play and Learn with Cereal O's* help children get a great start in life, so please spread the word to get this resource into the hands of parents, caregivers, and educators. A small effort on your part can give youngsters a more fulfilling childhood and a brighter future.